Believing Aloud

Believing Aloud

Reflections on Being Religious in the Public Square

MARK DOUGLAS

WITH A FOREWORD BY
Walter Brueggemann

CASCADE *Books* • Eugene, Oregon

BELIEVING ALOUD
Reflections on Being Religious in the Public Square

Cascade Books
An Imprint of Wipf and Stock Publishers
199 W. 8th Ave., Suite 3
Eugene, OR 97401

www.wipfandstock.com

ISBN 13: 978-1-60899-247-8

Cataloging-in-Publication data:

Douglas, Mark, 1966–.

Believing aloud : reflections on being religious in the public square / Mark Douglas; with a foreword by Walter Brueggemann.

xiv + 184 p. ; 23 cm. — Includes index.

ISBN 13: 978-1-60899-247-8

1. Religion and politics—United States—21st century. I. Brueggemann, Walter. II. Title.

BL65.P7 D68 2010

Manufactured in the U.S.A.

Contents

Foreword

The all-time winner for shrewd ethical reflection in quick, terse scope is Reinhold Niebuhr. He wrote some important books. But his relentless, defining work was the short essay in which he succinctly and clearly analyzed a public issue and drew a conclusion that helped us to see afresh and to ponder a fresh course of action. As I read the present essays, it occurred to me that Mark Douglas continues the work of Niebuhr, with the same shrewd discernment and sure-footed self-confidence. These essays, in sequence after those of Niebuhr, offer a succinct analysis and a freshness for both seeing and acting. I take the comparison to be a fine compliment for Douglas who is himself a "critical realist" after the same manner as Niebuhr.

But of course there are important differences between the ancient offers of Niebuhr and the contemporary thought of Douglas. The defining difference, I suggest, is that Niebuhr lived and worked while "the center held." (It has to be appropriate here to quote Auden, Niebuhr's great friend.) That is, he could count on some political and theological assumptions to be widely shared; for all his compelling radicality, he spoke from the center, elsewise he would never have made the cover of *Time* or been "the teacher of us all." That did not make his work any easier and he had plenty of distracters and adversaries with whom he contended.

But for Douglas, clearly the center does not hold; on every issue, "things fall apart." On the one hand, the division of right and left is unbearably acute on every issue; on the other hand, there is a common view of a failed public, so that there is not even a "center" from which or for which to contend. This means that Douglas is much more "on his own."

Except of course he is not. He is deeply situated both in critical ethical thought that is capable of sustained unflinching analysis and in the thick theological tradition of Christian reflection that brings certain insistences about God and neighbor to every pubic issue. That tradition of critical thought permits him to cut below the familiar cant that is everywhere available (witness Ann Coulter to whom he refers). The theological tradition that keeps our best discernment penultimate permits Douglas a wry whimsy about even the most urgent issues. As one pages through these essays, one can see how Douglas works from rootages, critical thought, and faithful affirmation. He never calls attention to those rootages, and permits the reader to take the argument without contesting those traditions that inform him. But whether those roots are recognized or not by the reader, it is exactly those linkages that permit Douglas to step outside the familiar and the expected to see differently.

Douglas spends a good bit of energy reflecting on what it means to be "secular," how one discerns and contends in "secular" context, and how one recapitulates a faith tradition in the midst of the "secular." Clearly he understands that "secular" need not be a closed ideology of "secularism" (a preferred characterization by "true believers"), but it is rather an open arena where faith traditions can have free play, as long as they do not seek to preempt the field. Douglas is willing and eager to have his say in the public square. He does not contend that the square is "naked" without explicit faith traditions, but one can see in his argument that he brings a thickness and a subtlety that one-dimensional rational positivism could never offer.

What strikes one consistently in these closely reasoned pages is that his brief but disciplined analysis helps one to see what one has not seen before. I would not say that this is "prophetic imagination," except to recognize that the ancient prophets re-imagined the world with reference to God. It was not without reason that Niebuhr was variously regarded as a prophet, and the point of such an identity for him was not his negativity about culture or his jeremiads, but rather his capacity to see differently and faithfully. In like manner Douglas is "prophetic" (though he might prefer to be a "wise man"), because he re-imagines what is in front of us that we thought we had already fully understood.

Thus he considers the "War on Christmas" and refuses to engage because Advent is for waiting and not for battling. He can push back against blustering right-wing politicos to exhibit their theological assumptions that are less than winsome. He can probe with equanimity the disappearance of newspapers and what that means for liberal democracy . . . though I suspect he owes us a few more pages on that subject now that the crisis is more acute than it was a few days ago when he wrote. He can connect U.S. policy toward Kenya with U.S. policy toward Israel, a linkage few of us would otherwise have noticed. He can consider the democratic dimension of March Madness, though I think he has not yet commented on the anti-democratic practice of the Football Bowl System. And who else would have seen that faithful vulnerability is a counter to the fierceness of fundamentalism? Or that "cultivating our discontentments" lets us love God and neighbor better and differently?

The sum of Douglas's thought is to make the world "strange" in a way that would delight the French theorists. But then, acknowledging such strangeness is a recognition that the world is laden with the inscrutable, that it belongs to God and not to us, that it is not and will not be on our own terms. The alternative, fostered by a culture of dumbing down, is that the world is familiar and can be mastered: in short, a practice of self-congratulatory idolatry that manifests itself in public policy. It surely is the work of the critical tradition, or of the theological tradition, or of the prophetic tradition where the critical and the theological converge, to make the world strange. Because such strangeness requires repentance, a coming to terms with what will not yield to us.

Mark Douglas has much more work to do, young and bright as he is. I will be glad, for instance, to have him continue his reflection on "the new world" of Obama, for the Bush administration made it perhaps too easy for him. But his work is not that of party, and he no doubt finds ample fodder for work in the midst of the new regime. I am very glad to have Mark as a colleague. His work is a gesture of assurance that in a world where things do indeed fall apart, the sweet convergence of faith and reasonableness can be sustained. One can deeply enjoy any one of his forays. But the sum of them is much more than enjoyment. It is disclosure; it is summons; it is assurance. It is all those things that mindless consumerism, funded by imperial ideology, does not want us to notice. Douglas's capacity to notice is a sustaining gift for us.

Niebuhr ends his "Preface and Apology" in *Leaves from a Notebook of a Tamed Cynic* by speaking of his vocation as a minister:

> I make no apology for being critical of what I love. No one wants a love which is based on illusion, and there is no reason why we should not love a profession and yet be critical of it.

Douglas clearly exhibits that practice of "love and criticism," love and criticism of our society and its economy, love and criticism of his faith. In the end, no doubt, he will come down in deep love for faith and maybe even for our U.S. culture. But he holds off for a while, a long while, showing us that criticism itself is an act of honest faith. His work is a continuation of that of Niebuhr, and even an echo of the more ancient Jeremiah. Let the reader beware!

Walter Brueggemann
Columbia Theological Seminary
December 2, 2009

Acknowledgments

This has been a peculiar book to write. Because I started writing the editorials well before the idea of a book came to mind, by the time I started to write what I thought of as a book, half of it—the editorial half—was already written. I've tried to be faithful to my musings on what I was trying to do while writing editorials as I had them. I am aware of several occasions, however, when I looked at an editorial written months earlier in light of what I was writing in a chapter and thought, "Is that why I wrote that???" They say hindsight is 20/20. More likely, hindsight is a really wonderful way to see the parts of the past that we want to see. Regardless of what my actual thoughts or motives may have been in writing the editorials—or, for that matter, of writing the chapters—I've tried to be as honest as I could manage. May the reflections herein be helpful to readers—and if not helpful, may they at least avoid brokering the kind of subconscious mendacity that can afflict our memories and damage our societies.

A book this peculiar probably warrants a peculiar set of acknowledgments. Perhaps one set of acknowledgments for those who helped me think and work while writing the editorials and another set for those who helped during the writing of the chapters. Or perhaps one set for those who dealt with the more secular matters that this book takes up (especially the editorials) and another set for those who dealt with the more "churchy" matters. In either case, the overlap between the two sets of acknowledgments would make reading cumbersome. So here is at least a partial list of those whose comments and thoughts shaped the whole of this book. As to whether these shaping forces helped or hindered, clarified or confused, defined or defiled its writing . . . well, that probably depends on who is reading this text and for what purposes. If the reader feels the need to locate the sources of either the strengths or the faults in this book though, I recommend blaming the following people:

Stephanie Ramage at *The Sunday Paper* had the courage to take that paper's editorial section in new directions and hire, among others, an academic and churchman—and then to support me, often patiently waiting for late-arriving editorials. Hopefully, she thinks her decision was not only courageous but wise. This taste of writing editorials not only whet my appetite to continue doing so in other contexts but helped me recognize just how much I would *not* want to make my living in the newspaper business. It's a tough industry and growing tougher. Regardless of what any of us may think of the quality of contemporary newsmedia, we should mix in at least a bit of sympathy and appreciation for those willing to make a profession of thinking aloud.

Cascade Books and its editors have been as important to the back end of this project as Stephanie and *The Sunday Paper* were to the front end. I'm grateful to this provocative new press for being willing to take up a project that doesn't exactly fit the usual formats or temperaments for a book. Thanks also go to Leslie Fuller, a very bright and careful student at Columbia Theological Seminary, for her work in compiling the index for this book.

Walter Brueggemann and David Bartlett have been invaluable colleagues at Columbia Theological Seminary and have modeled the type of collegiality that I aspire to inculcating in myself. Both of them read every editorial that I wrote—usually immediately after my writing it—and commented appreciatively and critically about each of them. Then they both read the entire manuscript and commented helpfully on it. And when I asked Walter to write the foreword for this book, he not only immediately agreed to do so but said such nice things about me and my work in it that he made me want to become the scholar he describes there.

I shared parts of chapter 2 with my colleagues in the Historical/ Doctrinal Area, Charlie Raynal and Marcia Riggs. Both offered sage advice about how to improve it. Then I shared parts of chapter 3 with a range of colleagues at C. T. S., whose stimulating conversation on it didn't so much reshape its parts as motivate me to continue into chapter 4 during a period when I had begun to bog down. C. T. S. has been a superb place to work and doesn't so much rebuild the faculty after senior colleagues retire as reload it with stimulating new colleagues.

I've presented aspects of this work to a wide range of clergy and laity, including folks at First Presbyterian Church, Auburn (AL)—where the first inklings of this book took form when I gave the Leith Lectures there— Rock Spring Presbyterian Church (Atlanta), First Presbyterian Church (Atlanta), Alpharetta Presbyterian Church (Alpharetta, GA), Second Presbyterian Church and Sandia Presbyterian Church (Albuquerque, NM), a group of young and very cool Presbyterian ministers and educators from around the U.S. who had gathered in Montreat, NC, and a large group of doctor of ministry students at C. T. S. in a class I taught on religious language in the public sphere. Hopefully, everyone that heard or read my halting attempts to describe what I was doing here will rush out and buy this book now.

While I was writing my editorials and reflecting on the ideas of this book, my friend and teacher Charles Mathewes published his book *A Theology of Public Engagement*. I can't begin to divide up the places in this book where his thoughts end and mine begin. His book is richer by far than this one. (Though it's also a book that demands riches to buy. Chuck writes great books but I wish he'd write less expensive ones.) Undoubtedly, some of the ideas in this book began in his brain—and they're probably the better and more fecund ideas. I'm glad he came to the University of Virginia before I left and seriously annoyed at how good he is at what we both do.

My wife, Lindsay Armstrong, has been a partner not only in life and parenting but in ministry. Watching her do her job—whether as a senior pastor or as an associate minister—consistently leaves me either in wonder or frustration (and far more of the former than the latter). John Milton thought that marriage was as much a matter of mental as physical chemistry. With a partner who is so good at both affirming and challenging me, I know he was right. Watching someone who is simultaneously so competent and so faithful in her work is a kind of grace. Thankfully, our daughter shows every sign of developing many of her mother's graces without inheriting too many of either of our vices. Their very presence spoils me.

As I was growing up in rural Colorado, my parents, Bruce and Bobbie Douglas, took me to church and talked about politics. If you'd told them then how passionate I'd become about a life caught up in both faith and politics now, I think they'd have been surprised. The vocational path I planned growing up and the actual vocation I now have are quite different. I think they also might wonder about the wisdom of their decisions then—especially since we've all moved in different directions with regard to both faith and politics over the past fifteen years (though each of us thinks that the others moved far more than we did). My suspicion is that they no longer think I know what I'm talking about with regard to either religion or politics—and this book may prove them right. Regardless of our differences in position and temperament, they taught me that these things matter and they have supported me in this surprising vocation of mine that combines both faith and public life. This book is dedicated to them.

Decatur, GA
March, 2010

1 An Invitation to Believe Aloud

I would be replacing Ann Coulter.

That's the thought that ultimately convinced me that I should take on the task of writing weekly editorials for a local newspaper. I didn't know whether I could produce something worth reading every week. Nor did I know whether my particular perspectives would be appreciated by readers regardless of whether I thought my work was worth their attention. I didn't even know whether I really had the time to commit to the work. But I knew that everyone who picked up a copy of *The Sunday Paper* would read my thoughts instead of Coulter's. That was enough to sway me: my opinions may or may not be worth much, but surely they were better than the malicious disdain and duplicity that she passes off as responsible editorializing.

So at least in part, that's why I got into the newspaper business. But how did I get into it? It began with a phone call.

In the summer of 2006, the Admissions Director at the seminary where I teach received the type of phone call that we get with surprising regularity: a local newspaper editor was looking for someone to respond to an editorial criticizing the world's religions as being the world's chief promoters of intolerance and ignorance. Our Admissions Director gave that editor my name and after they contacted me, I agreed to write up a 500-word response.

It wasn't an especially time- or thought-consuming task. Religion majors in college cut their teeth writing such papers, people of faith hear such criticisms regularly, and ethicists (my day job) generally like to argue. After an hour or so of work, I emailed my response off to the newspaper editor and thought no more of it.

That editor, Stephanie Ramage, liked the response. She called back a few weeks later to say that her newspaper was changing their editorial format, moving away from syndicated columnists and toward local talent

1

(her words). Would I be interested in being part of that "local talent" and writing weekly columns? We met once or twice for coffee, hammered out a few details (when columns would be due; how much and how often I would be paid; who would have the rights to reproduce them, etc.). I conferred briefly with my Dean of Faculty about taking on such a commitment (he agreed that it could be an interesting project but that it shouldn't get in the way of my regular work and such publications wouldn't count much toward promotion). I checked with my wife.

Then I said yes—for three reasons. First, this was a great (and rather unusual) opportunity to put my pen where my mouth was. I had already taught courses on the role of religion in the public sphere, published articles in academic journals arguing that pastors ought to think of themselves as public leaders, and generally encouraged my students to connect their vocational goals with the public good. What kind of hypocrite would I be if I didn't take up this opportunity to think publicly?

Second, like most people, I enjoy having my ego stroked. To be told that up to 350,000 of my fellow Atlantans would benefit from my wisdom certainly stroked my ego. The pay may have been pitiful, but oh, the prestige! Maybe this would be my stepping stone to national prominence! Maybe I would become one of those talking heads that show up on CNN—or better yet, *The Daily Show with Jon Stewart*! Maybe I'd be bathed in the adoration of a public eager for my wisdom! Or not.

And, third, as I noted above, it gave me great—and probably inordinate—pleasure to think that my words would replace those of Ann Coulter, whose vision of political responsibility I find reprehensible and whose opinions of her readers tend toward either cruelty or condescension. It was that thought that probably put me over the top in agreeing to write.

So, in the fall of 2006, I started writing weekly editorials for *The Sunday Paper*. A word about the newspaper's title: it's a name perfectly befitting a free weekly secular newspaper that comes out on Sundays and is for people to peruse with their morning cup of Starbucks. Invariably, though, the name confused people when I told them that I, an ethicist and ordained Presbyterian minister, wrote for it. Did I mean I was writing for the Sunday edition of Atlanta's large daily newspaper, *The Atlanta Journal-Constitution*? Or that I was writing for some peculiar little religious newspaper that comes out only when its coffers are deep enough to cover printing costs and is sustained only by the fervor of one or two people?

No. *The Sunday Paper* is a "we're in it for the profit" start-up newspaper of the sort that is reproducing like origami bunnies in urban areas. They have in-your-face cover stories, give attention to local events (especially odd ones), are filled with titillating pictures advertising various bodily augmentations (and the garments you can wear post-augmentation), and often include words you can't say in front of your five-year old. It's a peculiar place to find the thoughts of a theological ethicist, but then most places in which theological ethicists find themselves are peculiar.

Four of us would be writing editorials. Stephanie not only edited us but wrote a weekly column herself. She favored writing on the military, international politics, and the media. Her style was earnest, and her perspective rather fiercely independent. Bob, a retired professor of education, wrote on matters mostly related to schools and education. His columns were thoughtful though unsurprisingly didactic and tinged with nostalgia for the days before ideologies—from the left or right—got in the way of educators. Eric, a local morning DJ of the "Mutt and Jeff in the Morning" variety, wrote mostly about contemporary cultural politics; his DJ persona carried over into both his writing style and worldview, which tended toward Reaganesque conservativism. And I would write using a style that, in principle, tried to complicate issues without using complicated terms—which meant trying to get beyond, behind, or beneath popular arguments and their attendant dualisms (e.g., either left or right; either religious or secular; either understandable or abstract). In practice, it meant using far too many ellipses, em-dashes, and parenthetical statements. People told me to write more like Hemingway.

Stephanie gave me *carte blanche* to write on any topic I wished, which both pleased and surprised me. It pleased me because, like many ethicists, I'm a gadfly, both curious and easily bored, flitting from issue to issue. Writing on a wide variety of topics gave me the opportunity to reveal the limits of my understanding about all of them. That's not necessarily a bad thing, by the way: assumptions about the authority of experts, tendencies to confuse wisdom with technique, fears about being found ignorant or argumentative, and general sloth have combined to discourage otherwise thoughtful people from making public written arguments. In the face of the world's complexity, even the best ideas are imperfect and even the best writing maintains some vagueness. To attempt to write truthfully about the world always means bumping up against my cognitive limits. But as long as fresh ideas and public debate are the lifeblood of civil societies, it's better to be partly wrong and public than to refuse to engage the conversation. Or so I told myself every week when I worried that I'd be found a fool.

It surprised me because I figured I'd be asked to be the "religion beat" writer. Too many people think that a theologian is unlikely to be helpful in examining anything other than religion, just as people think that a philosopher is unlikely to be helpful in examining anything other than abstract ideas or a doctor is unlikely to be helpful in examining anything other than anatomy and physiology. And few people think that a theologian can contribute much to the conversations of a community that isn't composed simply of fellow-believers. Conventional wisdom—including the wisdom of quite a few people who study religion for a living—is that theologians carry too much confessional baggage into such conversations and that this baggage is likely to make theologians either unintelligible or unbelievable.

I didn't want to be the religion beat writer. Being of the opinion that a theological perspective is more a lens through which to view the world than a tool by which to dissect one of its parts, I wanted to write so as to give readers glimpses of the way theologians think and, in the process, reveal that we're neither gibbering idiots nor God-besotted ideologues. I wanted to reveal the relevance and helpfulness of a theological perspective. And Stephanie gave me the liberty to try to do just that.

I took the liberty Stephanie gave me as license and started writing on topics all over the place: popular culture, sports, health care, religion (which I'm more than happy to write about provided it's not *all* I have to write about), foreign affairs, Supreme Court decisions, civic leadership, electoral politics, etc. My problem wasn't that I couldn't find a topic of interest; it was that there were interesting topics everywhere I looked and it was hard to figure out which topics I was worthy of. I became the journalistic equivalent of a country bumpkin in the big city: wide-eyed and wondering how on earth I'd be able to describe what I saw.

That's not exactly a new place in which to find myself. Much of the work that I do involves trying to discern what is going on around me and trying to teach students to do the same: Who is acting and why? Who is being acted upon and how? What are the forces—conscious and not, individual and corporate, benevolent and malevolent—that are shaping those actions? And how might God be working in the middle of all of this? One of the things I discovered as I learned to write these editorials was what it must feel like to be one of my students, regularly trying to speak about topics on which I wasn't exhaustively informed using tools with which I was not entirely comfortable. The Socratic method I so regularly employ in teaching—lots of questions followed by further questions—can as easily degenerate into verbal harassment when applied to oneself as it can when addressed to others, especially when you feel the pressure of saying something meaningful to thousands of people in 800 words or less and you're working under a deadline.

Though I wrote on a wide range of subjects, I regularly found myself coming back to politics. Partly, I suppose, this was because in learning to write editorials, I found it helpful to read editorials and most editorials are about politics. Partly, this was because the political sphere never lacks for editorial fodder: opinion writers focus on politics because it's *easy* to do so. Partly, this was because the other matters I wrote on all had political manifestations. Mostly, though, I wrote about politics because political matters are, almost by definition, important matters. Politics, after all, is what you get when you put a bunch of people in a common space and ask them to figure out how to get along with each other and move forward in the world. To focus on politics is to focus on the means by which we live with each other. To write on topics in which there is political turmoil is to write about those times when we are having trouble living with each other.

My goal in writing about politics (to the extent that I had one and I was actually paying attention to it) was to express a way of thinking about politics that reaffirmed the idea that the deeply Christian virtues of faith, hope, and love not only *could* shape political vision, but actually *were* shaping it—no matter how distorted those virtues might be as they were expressed. Toward that end, I spent a lot of time trying to think my way out of the boxes of conventional opinion, if only because conventional opinion on all matters political has sadly degenerated into treating politics as a necessary evil by most and simply evil by some. And while I'll be the first to admit of the evil in politics, my theological training and religious inclinations have led me to adopt a very specific meaning of "evil" that doesn't accord with most of what most people mean by the word most of the time. So I wrote columns on why partisanship and bureaucracy are pretty good things, why most health-care debates are misplaced, why Christians shouldn't engage in culture wars, why liberals should want U.S. troops to stay in Iraq, and why those advocating for a return to state-sponsored prayers in public schools misunderstood the nature of schools, the public, and prayer. I tried to write editorials the way Emily Dickinson wrote poetry: by viewing the world on a slant.

Generally, then, I didn't write about religion in politics so much as give a religious vision of politics. In chapter 3, I try to describe that vision and show how I applied it. Making sense of chapter 3, though, might take a bit of space-clearing first. Not everyone thinks that religious language, concepts, and vision should be used in the already disorderly, confusing, and sadly shrinking space we call the "public sphere," lest it grow even more disorderly and confusing—or, even worse, be forced into some kind of oppressive orderliness through the power-backed demands of religious figures who reject the real confusions of the lived-in world in favor of the illusory clarity of moral certitude. So in chapter 2, I'll give a brief account of how I think religious language can work in the public sphere and why it might be valuable, even to those who don't share the same convictions as its speakers. And in chapter 4, in the process of describing some of the practices of "thinking aloud" as a religious person, I'll try to make a compelling argument about how religious thinkers should "think publicly" and why more media outlets would benefit by allowing them to think religiously. Or, to say all that a bit more concisely, chapter 2 is on why faith matters in the public sphere, chapter 3 is on what hope does to a vision of political engagement, and chapter 4 is on how love shapes the practices of "thinking publicly." Finally, chapter 5 will offer a brief argument for why we should practice faith, hope, and love—and why we shouldn't think we are doing something more than or other than *practicing* at them. Faith teaches us how to see the world; hope motivates us to act in the world; love shapes our actions towards the world; practice reminds us never to take ourselves too seriously while we're acting in faith, hope, and love.

On the one hand, the growing power of the blogosphere in politics would seem to make some of my arguments in those three chapters moot. Why publish in newspapers when newspapers are, themselves, disappearing? Why make arguments about how to talk when you can talk however you want? Why worry about the disappearing public sphere when its virtual replacement seems able to do so much more so much more easily? Such questions can give one pause.

On the other hand, it is precisely the power of the blogosphere, growing as it is at the same time that populist notions of democracy are, that might make this book useful. It isn't yet clear that internet-based media sources fulfill the same social and civic functions that newspapers have. Much like handing a sixteen-year old a list of errands and the keys to the car, we may be entrusting important obligations to persons just learning to use such powerful machinery in a responsible manner. So rather than invalidate the arguments in this book, attention to the growing power of the blogosphere might reveal the book's value: there are now far more people doing something like what I was trying to do in *The Sunday Paper* and some of them, at least, might find the thoughts herein useful. After all, once you account for the facts that that *The Sunday Paper* was as likely to be accessed via its internet site as a newsstand and that I was writing on just about whatever I wanted with my editor's blessing, there really wasn't much difference between what I was doing and what many bloggers do. It's just that I was slightly more (and more clearly) beholden to others than many bloggers and I got paid (a little bit) for my writing.

As I make my way through the arguments of the following chapters, I'll also include some reflections on what I discovered—about writing, about myself, about the public, and about living out a life of faith—as I wrote. If I've done it right, I may have convinced some of my readers—especially the less-religious types—that there is a richness to religious perspectives that often gets lost in the sound-bytes of big-name religious leaders. And if I've done it very well, I may even have convinced some others of my readers—especially the more-religious types—to take up the task of thinking and writing publicly, themselves. Because while a few writers have begun to do this fairly well (though they approach the task from very different perspectives; E. J. Dionne, Amy Sullivan, and Cal Thomas are examples), there are still far too few of them around, and as a result, American perspectives about religion tend to be malformed—which is a dangerous problem when religion continues to be a formative power in the lives of many within American society.

Those last few paragraphs make the book sound more abstract than I intend it to. Hopefully, readers will discover that as those ideas in the previous paragraphs are developed, they are less abstract than feared—though, possibly, not less complex than might be required to speak intelligibly in a complex world. To avoid such abstractions, I'll use a fair sampling of my columns as examples of what I'm writing about here. And the columns, at least, tended to be a bit clearer and less abstract than that last paragraph. (Indeed, over the course of a year, I was runner-up for a national prize for outstanding editorial and opinion writing—the *In Character Prize for Editorial and Opinion Writing*—which, whatever else it may mean, should at least mean my writing wasn't too mystifying.) Where I think a particular column illustrates an idea I'm describing in one of the chapters, I'll include an asterisk ("*") at the end of a sentence. The asterisk signals the existence of a representative column that can be found at the end of the chapter and exemplifies the idea at hand—like this: the editorials for which I was runner-up for the *In Character* Prize were "Give Me Patience Right Now!"* and "Waiting and Wanting, Part II."* So each chapter has two parts: the main body of text and a series of columns that model various ideas from that chapter.

The danger of using the columns as examples, of course, is that it will feel like saying, "What I meant to do here is . . . ," which is a little like explaining the punch line to a joke: if you have to explain it, either the joke wasn't worth telling or you didn't appreciate your audience. I'm not sure how to avoid that danger, though hopefully the various strengths and weaknesses of the columns, themselves, might mitigate readers' frustrations.

All things—good and bad—come to an end. My project of writing editorials for *The Sunday Paper* is no different. In February of 2008, Stephanie called me, audibly upset. The publishers of *The Sunday Paper* had decided to go a different direction and my columns weren't generating the kind of mail they hoped for. Against her wishes, they were letting me go.

They wanted to replace me with Ann Coulter.

Give Me Patience Right Now!

(Appeared December 24, 2006)

Recently, a woman in Rock Hill, South Carolina, had her twelve-year old son arrested by the police. His crime? He opened a Christmas present early. He was arrested for impatience.

That a twelve-year old should be impatient isn't surprising. The practices of delayed gratification are hard lessons to learn even without involving the police. Of course, actually calling the police on your twelve-year old is its own form of impatience: at wit's end over what to do with her unruly son, the Rock Hill mother pursued a course of action that seems to be driven by a desire to resolve all his disobedience at once. The problem, of course, is that twelve-year olds—whether they have a rap sheet or not—turn into thirteen-year olds rather than angels.

It's hard to damn her in isolation when the culture that surrounds her is, itself, so disinclined toward patience, though. And here, we almost need to get past the obvious and self-parodying examples without forgetting about them:

- The businessmen listening to the news on the car radio as they speed through school zones with a soda in one hand and Blackberry in the other on the way to jobs with companies that send all their mail via overnight delivery in order to compete in a lightening-paced global economy and thereby ensure the kind of market-share necessary to secure their fiscal future: faster travel, faster food, faster communications, faster money, and faster advancement all in an attempt to make fast their future.

- The environmentalists (who are rapidly replacing wild-eyed, corner-standing, sandwich-board wearers as the culture's chief doomsayers) keep making claims about what's going to happen to sea levels TOMORROW if we don't immediately control carbon emissions. And on the other side are all those who don't reduce, reuse, and recycle because it's inconvenient to walk those few extra steps to the recycle bin, drive a few miles less, or believe scientific study after scientific study on the causes and impact of greenhouse gasses.

- Those who crash-diet, fad-diet, and liposuction their way to the appearance of health because an actual healthy lifestyle (especially eating right and exercise) takes too big a chunk out of the day.

- The religious types who favor faith healers, rapture artists, preachers of prosperity, or heretics promising us our best life NOW (I'm sorry; wasn't that what Satan tempted Jesus with in the wilderness?) because the slow hard work of transformation and the demands of discipleship just take too much time.

And we think the actions of a frazzled South Carolinian are over the top? We're a culture of over-the-top responses and such responses—whether they involve calling the cops on your kid, administering shock and awe rather than doing the hard, boring, and admittedly uncertain work of torquing up diplomatic pressure as you allow weapons inspectors to continue their task, or damning a country to chaos and

its citizens to fear, death, and exile when it refuses to behave in the way you see fit—are all expressions of the refusal to wait.

It's not that our impatience is necessarily unreasonable. There are real needs, concerns, and threats that accompany us through life and are likely to call for fairly immediate response. Sometimes, we must admit, patience isn't a virtue so much as an avoidance of responsibility.

But how will we learn which times to respond and which times to wait if we never create the time necessary to learn the subtle processes of discernment that help us make such distinctions? Patience is a precondition (necessary though insufficient) for developing the kind of wisdom that can help us distinguish between (and deal with) the things we can prevent, the things we can mitigate, the things we must endure, and the things that will kill us. And since a disproportionate amount of what happens to us individually and collectively falls in that third category (and eventually we'll all come into contact with something in that fourth category), it makes sense to practice at patience now.

Christians—at least in principle—have been practicing at waiting now for a month of Sundays (not to mention two thousand years); Jews have been practicing at waiting even longer. And Jews and Christians are pikers compared to the faithful of many eastern religions. They haven't just been waiting, mind you: anyone can do that given a decent length of heavy rope and a chair to tie them in. They've been *practicing* at waiting. They've been trying to get better at patience in order to accrue the benefits that follow. And at least until tomorrow, kids all over the United States—excluding a certain twelve-year old in South Carolina—have been waiting as well. Maybe we can learn something from them?

There's much more to say in this column (and I'd really love to be done with it). But I can't begin a new section this far into the current column. I guess we'll have to wait until next week.

Waiting and Wanting, Part II
(December 31, 2006)

My nine-year old daughter wanted—and got—rollerblades for Christmas. It was a rather surprising wish, given that last year she wanted—and got—a skateboard and on the maiden voyage upon said board, she fell and broke her leg in three places. My wife and I justified the rollerblades by noting that: a) she's a year older, wiser and stronger; b) she's actually been rollerblading and isn't bad at it; c) we survived the broken leg incident; d) we like the "get back up on the horse that bucked you off" attitude; and, e) rollerblades were better than lots of the other things she's wanted in the past, including her own cell phone (as if), Bratz dolls (dressed like one of the girls Mayor Franklin is trying to get off the street), and a pony. Rollerblades, by comparison, are healthy, wholesome, and comparatively affordable. She's learning how to want.

Last week, I discussed the case of a South Carolina woman who had her twelve-year old son arrested for opening a Christmas present early, arguing that impatience has become a troubling marker of American society. But that case wasn't just about a refusal to wait; it was about how he (and his mother) wanted. He wanted his gift unreasonably; she wanted him punished improperly.

The ancients called this kind of inappropriate wanting "disordered desire." And there is certainly lots of evidence of disordered desires in contemporary society. One need think only of all the petty and tragic addictions redounding through society (drugs, sex, gambling, shopping, celebrity news, foreign oil, half-caf/skim milk cappuccino, etc.) to see such evidence.

But addictions are only the most obvious examples of disordered desire. Sometimes—though rarely, actually—we want bad things. More frequently, we want good things in bad ways—mostly wanting them too much (as is the case of most addictions) or too little. We want them in ways that preclude us from pursuing other good wants (as, e.g., preoccupations with health, safety, security, or liberty can do) or in ways that lead us to misunderstand the processes by which we achieve them (how's the whole "democracy in the Middle East" thing going?). And, hardest of all, sometimes we have wants that can't be satisfied (a different past, different genes) that we have to figure out how to live with without surrendering to stoicism or to the

addictions which we stuff into the hole such wants leave.

What has wanting to do with waiting? At least this: learning to understand, evaluate, and deal with our desires takes patience. We wait in order to give ourselves time to ask questions like, "Is this really what I want?" "Is this really what I should want?" and "How might wanting this shape my understanding of other wants I have?" And we have patience because we regularly surrender to the sharp jabs of wanting only to learn that what we thought we wanted turns out to not to satisfy (how many Christmas presents got returned this week?). Waiting, in other words, creates time for us to try to reorder our desires. And as we turn our backs on Christmas wanting and our faces towards New Year's resolutions (which are, after all, just different kinds of wanting), we're going to have to give ourselves time for the process of getting our desires reordered.

I have, thus far, been speaking rather existentially and homiletically (it's the last day of the year: what else do you expect from editorials right now?). So let me move from preaching to meddling and speak politically for a moment. Because while learning to wait and want may be important virtues in individual lives, they are foundational ones to the life of a liberal democratic state like the United States.

Liberal democratic states (which are the only kind of democratic states with any staying power) exist as one answer to a wager about how people should live with each other. The bet is whether a healthy and stable society is more likely to be composed of people working together to achieve a common goal or of people who put up with each other's different goals even when those goals conflict. The liberal democratic state puts its money—and its citizens' lives—on the latter position. Such a state prefers attention to procedures to focus on results, reform to revolution, and tolerance for disagreement to insistence on achieving agreement. It accepts the consequences of giving people the freedom to do bad under the assumption that this same freedom also makes it more possible for them to pursue what is good. And, as a result, it moves slowly and in ways that never fully satisfy any of its members—all of which mandates that those members learn to be patient and to order their desires. Everyone waits and wants; democracies ask their citizens to learn to wait and want in better ways.

As we peer over the edge of 2006 into a fraught new year, waiting and wanting may be hard things to do well—and the fact that we didn't do them very well over the last twelve months makes them that much harder—but perhaps actually attending to them may help. So be patient with each other and take the time to think about what you want and how you want it. The quality of our futures together may depend on it.

2 Being Faithful

I never pretended that I was a reporter. Why pretend? I never took anything that looked remotely like a class in journalism. I never worked on a newspaper staff—whether school paper or otherwise. I don't think like a reporter and, at least to judge from the eye-rolling I often get from my wife when I ask her to read something I've written, I certainly don't write like one. Fortunately, I wasn't asked to be a reporter. I was asked to be an editorialist. At the risk of oversimplifying the difference between being a reporter and being an editorialist, I was always clear that I had been asked to give my opinions on things, not to share data about them. And while there may be some basic rules of writing shared by editorialists and reporters (e. g., make sure you've covered the necessary "W's"—who, what, where, when, and why), there is one great advantage that editorialists have over reporters: namely, they need not repress or disguise their perspectives.

This isn't to say that reporters don't reveal their perspectives. There are dozens of ways reporters' perspectives are revealed, from the choice of stories and their placement in a newspaper to the types of questions they ask, the approaches they take to their stories, and the words they use (my rule of thumb: the more adjectives a reporter uses, the clearer that reporter's perspective). Likewise, there are editorialists who mask their perspectives behind data—which is usually a rhetorically clever way of getting readers to agree with their perspective, as if to say, "All this data can lead only to the following conclusion . . ." Really good editorialists may, on occasion, be able to use such a rhetorical device; most editorialists are not that good, however. I know I'm not that good.

I'm not even sure I'd use such a device if I were actually that good since I think real issues—the kind that are complex, meaningful, and sometimes seemingly intransigent—simply cannot be resolved merely by corralling all the data. On principle, I only wrote on issues in which

I could understand support for an opposing position no matter how strongly I disagreed with that position. I figured that if my job was actually to change other people's minds rather than either inflame them or reinforce the biases of those who agreed with me, I needed to be able to get inside those minds—to figure out what was motivating them, how they interpreted the data, and what they thought a compelling argument sounded like. As a result, I never wrote about some of the very issues (such as the death penalty) that are especially important to me. I just can't satisfactorily imagine a position other than my own. Not only did my sense of the ethics of editorial writing demand such a thing but the editorialists I most admired seemed to live by this principle. I think that's why I've always loved George Orwell's essays; he was so good at recognizing the appeal of the very things that he found most disturbing. And while I undoubtedly failed to live up to that principle, I think I can at least look back on my failed columns as failures—and recognizing them as failures helped me avoid making those particular mistakes again.

Unfortunately, the public craving for conflict tends to elevate some really bad editorialists who not only are outspokenly opinionated and unwilling to even countenance another position but who are more than willing to resort to name-calling or to disguise (or even replace) a few of the necessary "W's" if the data doesn't match their opinion. In a world seeking light, they prefer heat. I knew I wasn't a really good editorialist but at least I tried not to be a really bad one.

Moreover, it would have been hard to hide my perspective behind the mask of an everyman—someone whose opinion, once read, just seems to mesh with the thoughts and ideas of the readers, regardless of those readers' perspectives. I suppose that in part this is because ethicists tend to be controversialists. It's not that we're just an opinionated bunch—though, collectively, we may be—but because ethicists tend to take up issues about which there is substantive disagreement. Or, said differently, ethics usually gets interesting not when the questions are about right and wrong or good and bad but when they're about contending understandings of what is right or good.

The other reason it would be hard to hide my perspective is that it is distinctively religious. Whether by disposition, upbringing, academic training, some mysteriously activated "faith" gene, or purely the grace of God, I can make the most sense of the world when I view it through (hopefully informed) religious lenses. Although I do not always explicitly name or describe the way my faith shapes my worldview, my faith is there, subtly (and sometimes not so subtly) shaping my perspective. And since not everybody shares my faith—including many who belong to the same religious tradition I'm in—my perspective sometimes stands out. The impact of this faith perspective was never clearer than when I wrote on matters that were "religious and" matters—as in "religious and political" or "religious and cultural." Among the responses I received in response to my editorials, many were letters from fellow Christians who were surprised that even though my perspective was shaped by a faith tradition we shared, the conclusions I reached were quite different from theirs. My editorial "The War-on-Christmas Season,"* for example, elicited both criticism of the "you don't speak for me" variety (did I claim to?) and surprise of the "I never thought of it that way before" type. Given the relative paucity of actual responses I received during my time as an editorial writer (a paucity at least in relation to letters received by more outspoken editorialists), I was happy to receive either type of letter. The former appealed to the competitor in me; the latter to the teacher.

That matters of faith influence politics and culture—especially popular culture—is unsurprising. In the U.S., they have always done so. From the arrival of Pilgrims, Puritans, and Quakers before the country's founding to the continued influence of churches on laws (in many states you cannot buy alcohol on Sundays), on candidates (as when the religious right is courted as a voting bloc), on social welfare (think about all the money that is fed through churches to those in economic difficulties compared to that which passes through the government to them), and even on leisure time (regardless of what they call it, public schools schedule winter break to correspond to the Christmas season), religion and culture have always been inextricably and potently mixed.

This influence has had many benefits: promoting social stability, maintaining traditions of volunteerism and altruism, shaping political language, and enriching culture. Yet it hasn't been only beneficial. Religion, after all, has a long history of promoting division, rejecting wisdom, and exacerbating violence. Anyone who would speak religiously in the public sphere has the obligation of recognizing not only religion's benefits but its costs as well.

Indeed, attention to the dangers associated with religion's costs helped shape a tradition of secularism in the U.S., a defining aspect of which was to keep religious voices out of the public sphere or, at very least, to insist that religious people translate their religious language into one that could be understood by everyone. For centuries, political philosophers argued about the best ways to understand and maintain the distinction between the public and private spheres and to keep religion in the latter. A history of religious perspectives given public expression in the U.S. (e.g., during abolition and the civil rights movement) did little to shape the opinions of many secular philosophers that religion was quaint at best, for the weak-minded in general and the cause of atrocities on occasion. Given its potentially divisive impact, even the generously-minded tended to treat religion like strong medicine: to be administered only as needed and in small doses. Such were the arguments of secularism, anyway.

For quite a while it looked like the secularist argument was winning. Religious folk tended to respond either in reactionary ways or in agreement with secularism. They allowed the promoters of secularism to shape the argument. As a result even when they won particular battles (e. g., keeping a moment of silence in public schools, getting government vouchers for private schools), it still looked like they were fighting a rearguard action. In spite of the fact that fears of godlessness in American society have been around almost as long as there was such a place as America, during the 1960s and 70s it seemed that the forces of history were moving conclusively toward the victory of secularization and the dissolution of publicly valued religious authority in the West.

Which is not to say that there was no religious language in public settings. However, where religious language was being used—like printing "In God We Trust" on money and adding "under God" to the pledge of allegiance—it tended to be pretty innocuous language. It was a kind of "here's something we all agree on" approach that denied the actual disagreements that particular people of faith might have with each other and thereby significantly circumscribed the "we" who were agreeing—a kind of common-denominator approach to religious sentiment.

Indeed, one way to think about this kind of common-denominator faith is as the residue that remains after all the rich but clearly distinct religious languages have been pulverized and screened by the secularist project: it's what a universally shared (and therefore publicly accessible) faith language would sound like if such a thing could actually exist; a way of avoiding the perceived social costs that come with religious pluralism by denying that kind of pluralism a foothold in the public sphere.

However, there is no universally shared faith language (and arguments to the contrary actually prove that point since they, too, come from a particular and not universally shared perspective). Instead, as the variety of religions in the U.S. increased and the frustrations of people with particular religious perspectives grew, the arguments for secularization began to be drowned out by the cacophony of new and very distinct religious voices, each claiming the right to speak in their native tongues.

Before such an onslaught, it was almost inevitable that secularization would lose. And it did. Its chief proponents either died or changed their minds. Sympathetic political philosophers and theologians pointed to the double standard used to privatize religious perspectives while allowing various ideological perspectives into the increasingly pluralistic public sphere. Historians paid more attention to the benefits of religious voices in that sphere. Religious conservatives for whom secularization was a dirty word gained political power. An ascendant Republican Party threw their weight behind the project of establishing government grants for faith-based initiatives. Immigrant groups coming from non-secular states grew in number even as secular citizens in the West became more globalized and noticed the impact of religion to shape politics in, for example, Iran or Poland. And people everywhere in the U.S. looked around and noticed not only how religious the culture was but how frequently many of its citizens were willing to listen to religious perspectives at least in the name of tolerance. Secularity—or at least the arguments that undergirded it—fell out of style. Not everyone is happy about it, but for all intents and purposes, we now live in a post-secular world.

Public Religious Language After the Defeat of Secularization

Now it is (mostly) settled that faith matters in the public square—that religious thinkers neither have to leave their faith at the door when they enter the square nor translate their religious perspectives into a shared secular vernacular. There is common consent *that* faith matters in such a setting. But *why* and *how* faith matters is far less clear—and religious folk have done little to settle those questions.

By the time we were given permission to speak in our own idiomatic tongues, people of faith seemed to have forgotten how to talk in ways that were both faithful and publicly meaningful. Perhaps this is because we have been affected by the same trends that helped us gain admission into the public square (e.g., growing pluralism, the retrenchment of religion in and against society, the growing political power of religious conservatives, and closer attention to the way earlier generations of religious voices had spoken). Perhaps we had internalized the public/private split that marks secularization and had decided the most important matters we could talk about were internal ones (like whether or not to ordain gays and lesbians). Perhaps some of us entered the public square looking for a fight against secularists rather than seeking a new way to speak and be heard. And, as people so often do, perhaps we cut intellectual corners and tried to say simply things that are, by nature, complicated (much as the last few paragraphs did, having taken a complex set of arguments and boiled them down into a few broad stereotypes). The gags may be out of our mouths but we're awfully hoarse right now.

Continuing the secular preoccupation with resolving the problems of religious difference, people of faith have taken at least four approaches to religion in the public sphere after the defeat of secularization. The first of these has been to continue the project of shaping a common denominator faith, albeit one that is oriented more toward personal transformation than social stability. Religious language could be public language provided it spoke to everyone's situation, albeit in vague and aphoristic ways (a friend calls this "therapeutic deism"). Religious faith became faith in one's own project of self-fulfillment and religious language became the language of diffused spirituality (as in "I'm spiritual but not religious"). Where a common faith used to help maintain social stability, now it serves the ends of personal growth; projects of individual spiritual growth and personal wellbeing replaced those of communal growth and public welfare as the chief purposes of religious activity.

One need only watch *Oprah* to see this kind of common denominator spirituality and the way that it passes for religious attentiveness. It is religion-as-therapy, as if the primary purpose of religion were to make us feel better about ourselves (is it any wonder that *Dr. Phil* spun off of *Oprah*?). It's the kind of faith that appeals to everyone except adamant agnostics and hardnosed orthodox precisely because it is cozy enough to feel comfortable with and diffused enough to fit just about anyone. Its primary public manifestation is the self-help group and its basic prophetic pronouncement is, "We need to learn to get along with each other." Whether it has the resources to meaningfully address the real tragedies that make self-help groups necessary and the deep questions that are raised when we don't all get along with each other, however, is an entirely different story—a point I tried to make in "Tragic Theology."*

After all, the world religions with staying power haven't so much shaped themselves to fit human desires; they've asked human beings to shape their desires to fit within that tradition's vision of a spiritually and materially complex world. These religions aren't therapy (though many adherents find comfort in them) so much as challenges against too-comfortable and therefore easily falsifiable visions of the world. They may promise much but they also ask much of believers. Without a vision bigger than personal fulfillment and the resources to sustain that larger vision, this popular diffused spirituality will probably pass as quickly as it came.

At least from the perspective of developing a thriving public sphere, the sooner such an approach disappears, the better. The fear that discrepant religious languages would disrupt the robust conversations necessary for a thriving public sphere led to the development of an approach to religion that treated the public sphere principally as the location in which to share the pleasures of private spirituality. But it is almost certain that such an approach, which does little beyond preaching tolerance for diversity, fails to fuel those robust conversations. Tolerance and diversity are important, but they only become meaningful when we take seriously the perspectives of those who disagree with us, and common-denominator spirituality has been shaped to reject those very disagreements. Lacking either the motivation or the procedures necessary to address significant public differences, the spiritual-but-not-religious types retreat to their private spaces, unable to work up interest in much-needed public conversations. Ironically, the secular project has helped to bring about the very thing it feared: a diminished public sphere—though diminished not through uncontrolled antagonism but by personal apathy. Initially unwilling to be public without being religious, some religious folk discovered a way to be religious without being really public.

The second broad approach that people of faith have taken to engaging a post-secular public sphere has been to attempt to overcome the diversity of religious voices in that sphere by controlling it. The attacks have been two-pronged. One prong has accepted a vision of the world in which the state is the dominant player in politics and politics the dominant force in culture; they've attempted to foist their candidates upon the rest of us, to position themselves as close to the sources of political power as possible, and to speak as loudly as they can not so much in the public square as toward the halls of power. The other prong has recognized the degree to which culture precedes politics: they've attempted to make themselves arbiters of what is good or right in culture, to aggressively market their own products, and to co-opt the languages of other groups to their own purposes (e. g., "right to life" from the right and "freedom to marry" from the left—though how the languages of rights and freedoms fit Christian visions of why we care for others or how we understand covenantal commitments is left unclear). Jerry Falwell's "Moral Majority" may have helped initiate this approach but Pat Robertson (himself once a Presidential candidate) and the Christian Coalition have been dominant players in this approach, as most casual viewings of *The 700 Club"*(offered on Robertson's own special Christian television network, CBN) would attest.

In the process of attempting to refuse religious pluralism by overcoming it, these groups—from both the left and the right—have reduced their religious confessions to adherence to a set of political commitments and their religious identities to being members of a particular voting bloc. But at least for Christians, religious faith isn't principally about adherence to a set of commitments; it's about learning to live more fully before and toward God. And religious identity isn't principally about reducing oneself to a single category of identity; it's about discovering the mysteries of what it means to be created for relationship with God and others. Indeed, politics, itself, is about more than mere adherence to an agenda or reductionist identification with a party, so this approach is not only a bad way to be faithful, it's a bad way to engage politics—an argument I tried to make in "Faithful Politics?"*

Moreover, the effect of such an approach hasn't been to make the public sphere monolithic but to make it more contentious. It hasn't overcome a pluralistic culture so much as exacerbated divisions within culture. No wonder many people are uninterested in engaging in the conversations of the public square; they fear they're likely only to be yelled at. The very danger that most preoccupied those pursuing the secularist project came to pass—ironically, though, because attempting to keep religious voices silent in the public sphere meant religious people were rusty at speaking both faithfully and lovingly once they entered it. Yet this approach to engaging religiously in the public sphere, too, is likely to fail. Not recognizing the power of religious identity and action, it asks too little of its adherents; not recognizing the complexity of the world in which they act, it promises them too much in return. Whether out of a sense of boredom or betrayal, its adherents are likely to look elsewhere for clues about how to speak in the public square. Indeed, some of those in the vanguard of the religious right have turned away from politics for those very reasons.

The third approach that people of faith have taken to engaging the public sphere after the fall of secularism has been to ignore that fall. Having grown used to translating the language of their faith commitments into the vernacular of the public sphere, they carried on as if that vernacular were their native language. The groups that pursued such an approach have tended toward social activism, regularly making statements about the various economic, political, and social afflictions of the day—but always making those statements in largely non-religious terms. They might, for instance, express their support for a higher minimum wage by appealing to human dignity and economic stability rather than using the language of Christian love or adherence to divine commandments. Compare the social witness documents of most mainline Protestant denominations that are written on a wide range of socio-political issues (globalization, the death penalty, the environment, immigration, etc.) to those of many progressive secular organizations: you'll be hard pressed to see demonstrably different conclusions reached therein even if their starting points are dramatically different.

In part, their approach has been shaped by practical considerations: they regularly form coalitions with politically and socially similar groups from non-religious organizations or other religious traditions and the secular language of the public sphere has been helpful in keeping those coalitions focused on their objectives rather than on their constituent members. And, in part, their approach followed from their assumptions about what makes speech efficacious: they didn't want the broader public to trip over their language on the way to garnering that public's assent.

These were tactical considerations and, in themselves, are unproblematic. The danger with such an approach arose when these Christians returned to their churches and had trouble connecting the public vernacular that had grown comfortable on their tongues to the idiomatic language of the faith. Successful at being public, they struggled at being a church (or, occasionally, synagogue). One church I know of had a thriving ministry to the homeless that was supported by a wide range of individuals and civic organizations. Many of the people that attended the church came because of its social commitments but were fairly uninterested in the Christian faith. As a way of welcoming these people, the ministers and members downplayed the peculiar beliefs and activities of the faith. Over time, the church withered while the shelter they ran maintained its strength. The shelter still exists; the church closed its doors several years ago.

This approach to the use (or, more properly, non-use) of religious language in the public sphere may not have been especially helpful to believers but it hasn't done any immediate damage to that sphere. And many important social programs have been nourished by the socially active tendencies of many who took this approach. But it is an open question as to whether this approach can actually nourish the public sphere, itself, over the long run. If everyone expresses their commitments—faith and otherwise—by first translating them into a common language, where are the advantages that come with hearing different perspectives likely to come from? Would the public sphere really be better off if everyone *only* knew one way of talking about public matters? Certainly not. If Christians forget their native tongue, not only will they be unable to utter the faith commitments that only make sense in that tongue (and therein make them distinctly Christian), they'll be unable to provide a perspective that might, in its very differences from those other perspectives, prove to be publicly helpful.

These are three different approaches to using religious language in a post-secular public sphere. They do share at least two common tendencies, though. The first is that none of these approaches is especially informed by the theological commitments of the Christian faith. Giving a pass to questions about how faith might matter in the public sphere, they risk draining public discourse of the possibilities that might follow from the admission of faith-language into that discourse. Not asking *how* faith matters, they diminish the profundity of the recognition *that* faith matters. And, second, they share a preoccupation with the problems of religious pluralism. The first approach seeks a religious project that need not be pluralistic; the second seeks to overcome pluralism with a particular religious perspective; the third succumbs to the fears about pluralism that drove the secularist project in the first place.

The fourth approach to using religious language in the public sphere grows out of the fact that while most groups may think about the problems of pluralism that come with recognizing that we aren't all alike, some of us have long been clear that we aren't all alike. Minorities, especially racial-ethnic minorities, are reminded of difference every day. So where the earlier approaches were contending with the project of secularism and its collapse, this approach grew out of a different set of struggles, including having their visions of faith recognized by the majorities around them as authentically Christian. Unsurprisingly, distinctive traditions of religious speech grow out of those traditions associated with such minority groups. Take, as the clearest example of this distinctive style of preaching, prayer, and public speech, the black church tradition.

There is a kind of freedom that comes with having the distinctiveness of one's religious identity so readily on display, especially after the various civil rights movements of the latter half of the twentieth century. Black preachers are expected to sound like black preachers, whether they are preaching from the pulpit, calling out from the streets, or speaking at civic or political functions. We expect God to be invoked, the Bible to be affirmed, spirituals to be quoted, and connections to be made between whatever current situation we face and the situations faced by ancient Israel or the early church. When an African-American minister stands up to speak, our expectation that she will speak religiously functions as a loose kind of social permission-giving. Having already been socially located as "different" from the majority of society by virtue of the color of her skin and the U.S.'s legacy of racism, she feels less pressure to conform her speech to the way the majority of U.S. citizens assume religious people should talk in public.

Moreover, given not only the historic centrality of the black church in African-American communities and African-American ministers as community leaders but also the national commitment to include the perspectives of minorities on many social issues, African-American ministers tend to be invited to speak at civic occasions in numbers disproportionate to their actual numbers in U.S. society. So they are likely not only to feel greater freedom to speak religiously in public settings, they are often more likely to speak on such occasions. Indeed, one of the easiest ways to include religious language in a public setting—regardless of one's race—is to quote a spiritual. Or, better still, to include a gospel choir in the program.

However, as African-American minister friends have reminded me, this freedom comes at cost. Not only do they often face the assumption that they will speak in a particular religious way—which is peculiar as there are many ways that African-American ministers speak—but, when invited to speak, they are often given particular roles to fulfill: offer an invocation, speak about building social cohesion, offer the perspective of the black community. Fill the slot reserved for this particular kind of speech in this particular kind of setting. Fulfill our expectations about how you should speak; don't defy them. The effect of these assumptions is to reinforce a kind of conceptual segregation that replaces or supplements racial segregation. In this instance, we approve of particular religious language being used in full-throated ways—but in ways that allow for it to be cloistered off from the rest of our public conversations. Other racial/ethnic minorities face similar problems—as Korean and Brazilian pastor friends, among others, remind me.

Perhaps even more significantly, attention to the permission given racial/ethnic minorities to use religious language may be having the effect of encouraging persons who would otherwise identify themselves with a majority to signal their own embattled minority status. Thus, some Protestant groups who perceive themselves as facing dark and powerful "forces of secularization" have turned toward using the language of civil rights to defend their claims to the legitimacy of posting the Ten Commandments in courthouses and voting for candidates—or even running as candidates—*because* they share a common faith perspective. Turning their own particularity into a sign of oppression, they treat religious language as an occasion to promote a vision of their endangered distinctiveness or of a mystical national heritage at risk of being lost. That is, they conflate faith and faith talk with their identity as a member of a particular subculture and then fight to preserve that culture. Personally, I doubt whether such a conflation is adequate to deal with the complexities and interrelationships of faith, religious language, and culture, but that conversation is for another day. What is clear, though, is that such an approach risks gaining a clearer public religious voice only at the expense of allowing ones' identity to be reduced to a stereotype.

It could be that this particular approach to using religious language in the public sphere will recede from viability as the U.S. becomes increasingly multicultural and as closer attention to cultures, subcultures, and their relationship to identity reveal just how complex such things are.

Americans hardly live in a post-racial nation. They do, though, live in a nation in which matters of race are increasingly complex—as is pluralism in all its manifestations. It's unsurprising under such conditions that pluralism (religious and otherwise) is treated either as a threat or as a mask.

But what if we treated religious pluralism as neither a threat (as secularism and the religious agreement-by-domination perspective make it out to be) nor an epiphenomenal mask that hides a common faith (as the religion-as-therapy perspective makes it out to be)? What if we treated pluralism simply as a fact of life—a sign that people not only don't think alike when it comes to religious faith but that their commitments to those various faiths will inevitably shape their interactions with each other? What if the inevitable concerns that come with admitting many religious perspectives into the public sphere aren't so much problems to be resolved as conditions to be lived with, keeping in mind that the alternatives to living with those concerns (confusion, coercion, co-option) are worse? I treated my column as an experiment in thinking about how the particularity of a discrete faith tradition could coherently relate to a post-secular and religiously pluralistic culture.

Faith Faces Out

Treating my column as an experiment in how to think publicly and from a particular religious perspective meant using religious language where I thought it was appropriate. As a result, it also meant identifying myself as a particular kind of Christian in order to avoid promoting the illusion that my columns came from nowhere. Each week, there was a small picture of my face next to the editorial's title. With my face actually right there in the paper, I could hardly write as if I had no face. Sometimes—as in "The End of Culture Wars"*—I wrote quite explicitly as a Christian. At other times, my faith informed my column rather than sat as subject to it. But in all instances, I at least tried to think through the question, "How does my faith shape this column?"

Likewise, in the chapters of this book I swerve in and out of using first person pronouns and, in the process, connecting myself to the Christian faith and, thus, to the church. For some, this may be grammatically off-putting. For others, it may cause a bit of uneasiness of the type they might feel in reading someone else's mail. And for a few, it may produce some surprisingly intense (and possibly harsh) reactions: in naming myself as a particular kind of person, I simultaneously make myself into someone who is likely to be different from many readers—and facing difference can produce the kind of discomfort that can lead to strong reactions. (I would hasten to add that religious folk have not always done a very good job of being winsome in public, so reactions against religious identities in the public sphere are not entirely unjustified.) To the grammatically put-off, I apologize. Playing fast and loose with grammar is not only a sign that I'm not entirely clear on what I'm doing but also a not-especially-laudatory way I keep myself entertained while writing. To the uneasy, I offer a reminder you probably don't even need: though my approach to writing may be different than some, I really do write this way as a kind of invitation to you to keep reading and thinking on your own terms. And to those who react more strongly, I ask only for patience. Keep reading and decide at the end if your reactions are justified.

In coming face-to-face with the implications of particularity for be-lieving aloud—that faith doesn't exist in a generic flavor, that to write as a person of faith is to write as *this* particular person with *this* particular understanding of her own faith—a writer quickly discovers both new freedoms and new responsibilities. The freedom side of the equation is wonderful: no more paralysis-inducing obligation to try to speak like ev-eryone else when everyone else speaks with such a wide variety of accents; no subtly preoccupying concern that you must either represent everyone with whom you claim allegiance or allow your work to contribute to the project of enforcing the appearance of unity; no more leaving behind the parts of your thought, your faith, and your self that you most appreciate for making you you. Particularity brings relief.

The protean responsibility that is implied by the recognition of par-ticularity, though, is that Christians can't rely on widely-shared assump-tions about why *this* faith should face outward. The common defenses of such a project (e.g., that it's one's right to carry faith into the public sphere, that robust conversations in the public sphere make it—and therefore society—stronger, that if we don't establish a common faith language we may have to deal with a very peculiar one instead) don't necessarily bear any causal or determinate relation to the reasons that are internal to that faith. Why should the Christian faith face outward? How should Christians understand particularity? Or, more awkwardly if accurately asked, are there Christian reasons that we should act as Christians in the public?

Part of the answer to such questions is biblical. From the creation stories of Genesis on throughout the Bible there is a constant refrain that faith has implications for how we ought to live with others. Whether focused on matters of justice (Moses before Pharaoh, the warnings and promises of the Old Testament prophets, Jesus' command to care for the "least of these"), righteousness (Abraham's hospitality to angelic visitors, Job's dealings with his so-called "comforters," Paul's call to submit to secular authorities), or witness (Israel's call to be a blessing to the nations, Jesus delivering the Sermon on the Mount to the gathered crowds, Peter preaching in the marketplace), the refrain is clear: the Bible does not support a "just God and me" faith. (A side-note: many Christians would argue that those three—doing justice, pursuing righteousness, being witnesses—are all of a piece and, ultimately, joined together in worship and praise. That argument is a bit bigger than I want to advance here, however.)

Part of the answer to those questions is historical. In the long history of the church, it has always been most relevant when facing outward. Sometimes that relevance has been less-than-laudatory: scandals like the Crusades and missionary endeavors less interested in sharing the gospel than in obliterating indigenous cultures for their own advantages have certainly had a significant historical impact even if that impact has been widely destructive. But the church's outward focus has also shaped profound—and profoundly good—movements in history. It has established countless charitable organizations, hospitals, and support services. It has led fights against slavery, segregation, apartheid, and totalitarian governments. It has built schools, led literacy movements, and run after-school programs. It has dug wells, built houses, and worked to make them homes. It has built hospice programs and cared for both the dead and those who grieve after them. It has lobbied for more just laws and on behalf of the under- or unrepresented. One would be hard pressed to find any part of the globe that the church has not reached and, in reaching it, done good works. The church faces outward because it has always understood itself as sent outward to love its neighbors.

Part of the answer to those questions is evangelical. Unlike Judaism in which one is Jewish because one's parents are or the eastern religions (e. g., Hinduism or Buddhism) which claim that everyone participates in the cycle of birth and reincarnation whether they follow the teachings of those faiths in any particular incarnation or not, the Christian faith has consistently held that becoming a Christian is a matter of conversion or transformation, not natural processes. One becomes Christian by re-birth; not by birth. Even our children do not fully become members of the church until they can willingly make their own faith statements. As such, the church must face outward toward the world because that is where it finds its new members. (Incidentally: the claim that our own children are, at least initially, outsiders to the church ought to contribute toward undermining any comfortable claims from within the church about how it needs to be kept apart from "the world." We *all* begin as outsiders to the church and, at least this side of eternity, none of us can fully escape the concerns and trappings of the world into the cloistered protection of the church. Nor, I would argue, ought we or need we try.)

Part of the answer to those questions is doxological. Believing that God is the primary audience for all their actions, Christians practice at seeing everything they do as acts of worship. As such, they struggle *against* making too much sense of a world that can be neatly divided between matters that are "public" and matters that are "private." In a way, they recognize that everything they do has a public: the God whom they seek to glorify in their actions. Obviously, this doesn't mean that they can't understand or value actions that ought to be protected from interference by others in the community or the state. At a political level, Christians, as much as any group, see the importance of preserving and maintaining such space. But at a fundamental level—at an existential level—Christians live their lives before God and, as such, properly ought to refuse to let the distinction between public and private go all the way down. The wor-ship—praise, confession, thanksgiving, supplication—that shapes their whole lives will necessarily occur both in politically public and politically private spaces and thereby undermine claims that put too much emphasis on keeping public and private apart.

Surrounding these partial answers that come from Scripture, history, evangelism, and worship, though, is a more basic theological claim about why the Christian faith must face outward. It is this: we Christians cannot make sense of our faith without seeing the world as a sphere of divine activity and we cannot make sense of ourselves without trying to discern how God's activity in the world is both shaping and encouraging our own actions in it. That is, the Christian faith is incoherent apart from its most basic claim that God interacts with the world he has created, most especially through his incarnation in Jesus of Nazareth and his continued presence through the workings of the Holy Spirit. The church must face outward—it must be public—because that is where it finds and is empowered to respond to its Lord. If, as St. Anselm argued, faith seeks understanding, then it must seek it—at least in part—by looking outward.

As we go out, Christians will discover (much as we have always discovered) our neighbors, whom we have been commanded and enabled to love. Those neighbors will not be like us. They will have different faiths, different worldviews, different opinions, and different values. Undoubtedly, contact with those differences will create tensions. But at the same time, it will also put us in places where we can see a new revelation or hear a fresh word from the God who is at work in the world, often through those very neighbors. The understanding that faith seeks isn't simply about knowledge but about wisdom of the type that can come only through relationships with God and those she has created.

While it's possible to imagine Christians facing outward without speaking out, it's hard to imagine that being a particularly faithful activity. Pithy aphorisms like "In the church share Christ's love; in the world show Christ's love" or "Bear witness to Christ's love everywhere—and in the church, use words" may feel right to many of us but their very comfort ought to be disquieting. Such aphorisms give us permission to avoid doing something many of us would rather not do anyway without wondering what our lack of desire reveals when all-too-often it reveals that we're choosing the paths of least resistance. Not speaking—not having to offer explanations or make arguments—is not only a way of avoiding thinking about whether we might be asked to say something, it's a way of refusing to make ourselves vulnerable to the questions and arguments of others. But if we actually believe that we are shaped by and for relationships—that we become who we are being called to be through our relationships with God and others—and if we recognize that language-use is the primary means by which we relate to others, then refusing to speak and write in public is a kind of bad faith. It's a refusal to share who we are and to discover who others are in the process. Using words is simply what we do. So the question isn't whether to speak in the public or not; it's how to do so. What drives our speech and what forms should it take?

In chapter 4, I'll return to the topic of love and the mysterious ways that love and wisdom comingle as we learn to love God and neighbor and, thereby, grow in faith. For now, though, having made an admittedly cursory argument about why Christians ought to understand their faith as something public, I turn to the question of what I learned about an outward-facing faith as I wrote weekly editorials for a non-religious newspaper—about what happened as I experimented with believing aloud.

Writing Like I Believed What I Wrote

I was lucky to have the chance to write a weekly column and *The Sunday Paper*—and Stephanie, my editor—was courageous enough to hire a theological ethicist to write for it. It would have been simpler for everyone if *The Sunday Paper* had stuck with the syndicated columnists, all of whom played by the rules of typical editorial writing, including rules about how to talk and think about religious matters. I didn't even know those rules—which was, perhaps, to my advantage, since it meant I never really worried about the implications of breaking them.

I did know, though, that I rarely read anyone writing from the perspective of their own faith. On those occasions on which I did, I even more rarely felt like that perspective meshed with mine. That wouldn't be so troubling if weren't for the fact that I place myself squarely in the middle of one of the most mainstream traditions in Protestantism, which is, itself, the dominant religious perspective in the U.S. Since my suspicion was that these absences had as much to do with Christians learning to speak in the public sphere as with media obligations or audience biases, I decided to write from my faith perspective. Not *about* it, mind you; I certainly wasn't interested in writing about myself. But *from* it—to explore before a wide public the implications of what I confessed in church.

From the very beginning of writing the weekly column, then, I was faced with two deceptively complex questions. First, if religious folks really think that their faith shapes the way they understand the world (even if they are still learning to speak from the contexts of their particular faith traditions about the world) and if I'm one of those folks, then what guidelines would I follow as I tried to communicate? And, second, what might the process of writing the columns teach about how to believe aloud?

The guidelines I chose to follow were fairly simple. I wasn't trying to convert anyone to the faith (in my Reformed understanding of the faith, God converts people, anyway) so I wouldn't try to cast Christianity in only the best possible light. I wasn't trying to convert anyone to my opinion (I wanted people to think, not agree) so I would do my best to treat my readers as capable of thinking for themselves. And I wasn't trying to convert anyone into joining a cult of personality that revolved around me (I'd make a very poor object of worship, anyway) so I wouldn't try to show my professional and intellectual *bona fides* off by using unnecessarily big words, drawing on unfamiliar references, or hiding behind convoluted arguments.

That said, I do think that Christianity—or, more accurately, the God revealed in Jesus Christ and worshipped by Christians—comes off pretty well if left to itself, so I challenged arguments I thought were weak, as I did in "A Job For Today."*—an article I probably wouldn't have written had my editor not asked me to. I think some (well, most) of my opinions are pretty well founded and worth defending so I was happy to make my case pretty strongly. And I think that using the right big word or remote reference increases rather than diminishes clarity and that some arguments simply are complex. In a wired world, how hard can it be to look something up? My very first column, "Elegy for the Daily Paper,"* included a reference to Procrustes' bed (google it if you need to). I imagine I betrayed every one of those guidelines at one point or another—especially the last one. But they were still helpful to have. Moreover, they grew more refined as I learned from the time spent writing columns.

More interesting than the guidelines were some of the things I learned (or had reaffirmed) from the process of writing the column. And while I learned them by trying to write from a particular religious perspective, I think they can be generalized into insights for the many people who feel the obligation or call to face their faith outward toward the rest of the world.

The first lesson I learned was that religious language was tolerated quite well by most people. Of course, tolerance is both boon and bane. On the one hand, being tolerated meant not having to fight the battle of being accepted: readers were generally comfortable with the words I used. On the other hand, being tolerated meant that I was more likely to face indifference than resistance. Within the realm of editorial writing, being ignored is probably worse than being opposed; I imagine that this was one of the contributing factors that led the publisher of *The Sunday Paper* into the decision to let me go.

It's possible that my religious language was tolerated because I live in the South. There's just more religious language—and a lot more religion—

here than in the west where I grew up. As Flannery O'Connor once noted, the South may not be Christ-centered, but it's certainly Christ-haunted. On the other hand, I live in (and *The Sunday Paper* is written toward) Atlanta, which, like most urban centers, is more liberal, cosmopolitan, and pluralistic than the surrounding counties. Moreover, the dominant flavors of Christianity—even in Atlanta—tend toward the so-called "Free Churches" (Baptist, Pentecostal, etc.) and toward conservativism. G. K. Chesterton once remarked that in America, even the Catholics are Protestant. In the South, even the Catholics are Southern Baptist. Since I get my bearings from the Reformed rather than Free Church tradition, what I wrote seldom aligned very clearly with those dominant flavors.

I suspect, however, that my religious language was tolerated primarily because people didn't know what else to do with it. In such an openly pluralistic and materially well-off culture, the principle threat to a religious language isn't that it will be suppressed but that it will be ignored. It would follow, then, that the principle threat that particular religious languages pose to a large and openly pluralistic culture like that in the U.S. isn't that they will cause division but that they will contribute to its general apathy. We risk becoming Balkanized not through battles but boredom.

When citizens treat the perspectives of other members of the society as if they have no bearing on their own lives and thoughts, the results might be no less dangerous to that society than if they treated them as threats. There might be less violence and strife (at least for a while), but the gradual and insidious process of ignoring our neighbors is no less likely to lead to social destruction than open conflict—especially since one of the better ways to promote a violently self-destructive society is to give license to the idea that those around us are not so much neighbors to whom we have obligations as strangers against whom we must assert ourselves. And ignoring those around us is one way to avoid those obligations and tacitly reinforce our self-absorbed priorities for our own lives.

The members of American society, after all, have become fairly practiced at ignoring things. We have to. We live in a shopping mall society where dozens of products manufactured by myriad companies and sold in countless stores all perform the same basic functions (whether keeping our teeth sparkling, our bellies filled, our clothes clean, or our society mobile). And in such a society, we have to become adept at ignoring what else is out there in order to make it through our days using the things we are familiar with. In a technologically sophisticated society in which news from around the world (via countless internet, television, and print mediums) is delivered almost instantly to our homes and offices—much of which is troubling and most of which we can do nothing about—we have become quite good at averting our eyes in order to sleep at night. In a globally mobile society in which the others in our communities are as likely to come from some other part of the world and be gone in only a few years as we, ourselves, are to move in pursuit of a job, a lover, or a dream, we have become proficient at avoiding eye-contact or being on a first-name basis with our neighbors in order to save the efforts involved in building transient relationships and the pains in saying goodbye. We ignore the world around us not because we don't care but as a kind of coping mechanism that saves us from having to care too much about too many things. Apathy in the U.S. is as much a mode of personal protection as a sign of declining civility.

If attentiveness is a bigger problem than conflict, then editorial writing—especially from a religious point of view—probably ought to be more concerned about catching peoples' interest than in trying not to offend or confuse them by using religious language. I think this may be why so much editorial writing is so long on confrontation and so short on substance. Conflict—especially when we can observe it from a safe distance—is attractive in the most literal sense: it draws our attention. Where secularists were worried about the problems of understanding each other if we didn't speak a common language, I tended to worry more about the problems of our not being interested in each other and to think that concerns about comprehension were overblown (after all, there are quite a few agnostics and atheists who seem to understand what religious people are saying even if they don't agree with them). My concerns about using religious language weren't epistemological; they were aesthetic. And to judge from the range of letters and emails I received, my concerns (and assumptions) were at least somewhat justified.

I suppose that's the second thing I learned while writing weekly editorials: that people are more interested in attractive (again, in the literal sense of the word) arguments than clear ones. That's not to say that I aimed at ambiguity or vagueness—though such things are likely in trying to make sense of a complex world. Instead, I tried to offer surprising connections (like comparing Kenya to Israel in "Q&A"* or making a hopefully serious point by way of reviewing *Spiderman 3* in "Saying

Something Important"*). And, as I hope both those editorials make clear, using explicitly religious language doesn't necessarily distract from an argument; it can clarify it.

Of course not all religious arguments are clarifying. A couple times I took on religious arguments I thought were pretty shoddy (as in the previously mentioned "A Job for Today") or that I thought distorted the very faith they intended to affirm (as in the previously mentioned "Faithful Politics?"). Just because I wasn't the "religious beat" writer didn't mean I wasn't interested in writing about religion! Since I think that religion has a great deal of impact on most cultures—including that of the U.S.—it's natural that I'd make frequent connections to religion in my articles. I probably wrote more about religion than most editorialists who have been given as free a hand as I had, and not just because that's what I study and teach but because I think it matters (which is, in part, I suppose, why I study and teach it).

There are lots of religious arguments out there and they aren't all of the same value. Moreover, since our cultural religious literacy is pretty pathetic, not many folks have developed the tools to distinguish between good religious arguments and bad ones. And the worst offenders in the competition to be the worst at distinguishing between good and bad religious arguments tend to be religious folk. It's as if we religious types are so pleased to see our faith recognized that we fail to recognize that some expressions of our faith aren't that good. We react, for example, as if "Christian" were an adjective describing a virtue rather than a person, place, or idea. I got compliments sometimes for the wrong things (either on pretty weak editorials or on a point somebody would read into an article that I not only didn't make but wouldn't make if I'd been writing on that topic). And I got criticisms that left me scratching my head as to how anyone could possibly have drawn *that* conclusion from what I'd written. For most preachers, this is pretty familiar terrain: people—especially the ones who are only halfway paying attention—hear what they want to hear. Indeed, sometimes it feels like the wonder isn't that religious people can communicate with people who don't share their faith; it's that they can communicate with people who nominally do!

So my presumption that the problems with public religious arguments have more to do with aesthetics than epistemology doesn't mean that all attempts at attraction are good. As car accident rubbernecking, tabloid voyeurism, and Ultimate Fighting bloodlust reveals, we can be attracted to the tragic, the tragicomic, and the violent. As much as any of our faculties, our aesthetic sensibilities need to be developed; as much as any other actions we undertake, our attempts to communicate with others need to be trained. For Christians, at least, that faculty is shaped by hope and those actions by love—virtues which we'll explore more closely in subsequent chapters.

My conviction that the tensions of using religious language in the public sphere have more to do with aesthetics than epistemology bore fruit in one surprising way: it helped me look differently at the discord that religious language so often produces there. When we assume that discord is the product of our failure to understand each other, we tend to assume that the source of our disagreements lies in the faulty reasoning of one of the parties involved and we try to address the problem either by convincing that other party that we are right or silencing that other party by insisting that they use our dialect. And we see the end result—lots of yelling at each other, at least to judge from many of the more vituperative arguments about religious perspectives on public issues that we see around us—as evidence of the other side's irrationality.

If, however, we think of those tensions as driven by aesthetic concerns, we might see all the yelling not as a sign of the depth of our disagreement but as a signal that we fear being ignored. We argue not because we refuse to agree but because those arguments remind us that we matter. Instead of being the means by which we communicate the things that are meaningful in our lives, those arguments morph into the source of that meaning. We rely on an argument's ability to make us "attractive" (again, in the literal sense) to others. And if that's the case, we can't solve the disagreement by either producing convincing arguments or insisting that our opponents use a different language.

Instead we either find a better way to make our arguments or we accept the fact that we won't agree and try to figure out how to live with each other in spite of our disagreement. Doing the former will take some imagination on our parts. Doing the latter will take not only imagination but finding a way to see—and signify to them—that our opponents lead meaningful lives. In either case, we'll have to pay closer attention to what makes our arguments attractive, which means paying closer attention to aesthetics. As I wrote, I tried to regularly remind myself: it's not about comprehension. It's about meaning.

The priority I gave to aesthetics suggests a different way for religious people to think about language-use in the public sphere. Rather than being preoccupied by either translating their faith-language into a common vernacular or maintaining the confessional integrity of that language in the face of calls for translation, religious folks would be just as well served to think about their public language-use in practical ways. Sometimes using confessional language makes more sense—as, for example, when trying to make a faith-claim about a civic religious dispute. Other times it makes more sense to attempt to translate their faith language into a more widely accessible vernacular. In either case, the question "What is the most effective way to write about this matter?" is wedded to the question, "What effect do I intend this writing to have?"

But why allow practicality to trump particularity when it comes to the words we use? Although there may be a range of answers to that question (e.g., to become conversant in many dialects; to avoid unnecessarily offending others; to prevent becoming too wed to any particular set of words), my basic answer—the answer on which I relied when I was asking myself how to say what I wanted to say—has been that Christians, at least, don't understand the words that we use as ultimately determining the way the ideas those words convey are received. We won't—indeed, we can't—get our words right. Instead, we rely on God to gracefully use our faulty words as a means through which his purposes and wisdom are conveyed. (I suppose this is an instance in which being a preacher actually helps in the process of believing in public. Preachers—at least the self-aware ones—are intimately aware of the limits of their own words and regularly surprised by the possibilities that those limited words give rise to.) If we can't get our words right, then we don't face the burden of saying the "right" thing and we can learn to live into the freedom of using the words that seem most appropriate for our varied purposes.

The third lesson I learned is that wisdom is where you find it. I regularly read my "go to" writers while looking for help in shaping an idea. Most of the time they were helpful—but not always. Sometimes I ended up being most helped by reading someone with whom I often disagreed. Usually that was because such a writer helped me better understand the nature or source of our disagreement. Sometimes, though, they helped me by revealing the flaws in my own thought. Mostly I noticed these flaws while walking the dog in the morning—which, surprisingly (at least to me) was where I did some of my better thinking.

It's an ego-bruising experience to be corrected by someone with whom one usually disagrees. I usually fought against such corrections for as long as I could in order to avoid such bruising. I would brood and sulk and occasionally talk to myself while dealing with such correction. I don't imagine I was much fun to live with at those times. At least one member of our family benefitted from that kind of ego-bruising, though: the dog tended to get brisker and longer walks on those days when I was revising my thoughts.

More often, though, wisdom came from unexpected places: a publication about the findings of a new study in an area of research with which I was unfamiliar, a jolting reminder that the settled understandings of history are far less settled than I imagined, a conversation with a guy at the gym who has stopped voting because he's frustrated by the populist impulse shaping so much of American politics. (See "Oh Happy Day"* and "When the Problem is the Problem"* for illustrations of what happened when I stumbled across a new study and when I was reminded of the power of history, respectively). That wisdom comes from unexpected places should be unsurprising to a guy who thinks you have to look out into the world to see how God is acting. It kept surprising me, though, at just how good wisdom was at sneaking up behind me and whispering "gotcha!" in my ear as it tickled my mind. There is something distinctly pleasurable about feeling a light bulb in your brain suddenly turn on; at least for me, it was a semi-regular hint that God had more revealing to do than I'd thus far experienced.

Which brings me to the fourth and, for the purposes of this chapter at least, the last thing I learned (or, rather, am still learning) in the process of believing aloud: revelation both shapes and is shaped by faith. On the one hand, the shock of a revelation always pointed to something unfinished about my own life and faith. Far from feeling like my mind was a repository of accumulated wisdom into which I would weekly wander in order to find the next gem to share with readers, I tended to have an intuition about a particular topic that I couldn't give voice to until I was actually writing because I didn't really know what I thought about that topic until I was connected to the keyboard. Then, while sitting there at the keyboard, I had to figure out how to interpret whatever discovery I had stumbled across even as I was describing it. So each week—or at least the weeks when I discovered something—was a reminder that I must not be done learning.

Moreover, since I tried to carry my faith-formed sense of things into editorial writing, those discoveries were reminders that my faith wasn't complete either. St. Anselm talked about "faith seeking understanding," which, I guess, is what mine was doing. Implicit in Anselm's statement is the recognition that faith is neither a discrete body of special knowledge nor a reassuring foundation onto which one might strap oneself to avoid being swept away by the whirl of the world. Faith may (well, must, really) involve knowledge, but since it is a gift that is never entirely in our control sometimes faith means being willing to face something mysterious. Faith can be stabilizing, but since it doesn't originate in us it also reminds us not to trust too much the very places in which we most want to feel secure. If anything, thinking of faith as a kind of special knowledge or a source of unwavering constancy is antithetical to Christian faith because such emphases treat it as something that, once we have it, we *have* it, as if it's a thing which we can wrap around ourselves as a buffer between ourselves and the world rather than as the goad that sends us out into the world seeking after wisdom.

One way I tried to keep this understanding of faith in mind—to be faithful to faith—was to avoid writing only on the topics about which I felt the greatest expertise. Obviously, I chose topics that I felt some comfort with (religion and politics, war and peace) and avoided topics I didn't feel equipped to explore (international banking, city planning—though I also avoided those topics partly because I didn't want to reveal myself as an utter fool), but I also avoided a few topics that I felt very comfortable with (euthanasia, ecclesial politics), if only because I would only be rehashing arguments I'd stopped having. This approach led to some nervous moments as I watched a deadline looming while trying to prepare myself for an insight I didn't yet have and even more nervous moments after I sent articles off and was left wondering whether I'd interpreted my inspiration properly or whether I'd get slammed for missing an important and fairly obvious problem with my argument. For the most part, though, I got things in on time and without too much post-publication bruising. Maybe that just proves I wasn't trying hard enough at seeing something new. I hope not. I'd like to think that my faith was being shaped by those moments of revelation.

On the other hand, though, my faith clearly shaped those revelations. Having spent years in training myself to think and to believe, I carried a fairly well developed set of commitments into those moments of inspiration. I used those commitments to help me interpret what those revelations meant. Maybe I wasn't done learning but I couldn't ignore what I had already learned—nor would I have chosen to even if I could. It's not just that I carried prejudices into my processes of interpretation. It's that some of those prejudices weren't so much the product of pre-reflective bias as they were the content of post-reflective conclusions. Part of my task as an editorial writer, as a Christian, and as a human being, has been to move those biases from the former category into the latter. I'd like to think along the way that in the process of reading what I'd written, other people's biases moved in the same direction. They may not have agreed with me but at least, perhaps, they could give better reasons for their disagreements.

The upshot of all of this reflection on the relation between revelation and faith has been, I think, this: that writing editorials did more than give me a chance to experiment with the processes of speaking from faith. It actually changed my faith. Not in dramatic ways. I didn't convert to another religion or even another denomination. I did, however, experience my faith as continuing to undergo the project of being converted into something deeper and freer and more provocative that even now I'm not sure how to name. Writing editorials became a spiritual discipline for me because each week I was reminded that neither I nor my faith was completed yet—that the lifelong project of breaking down the disorders in my life and faith and establishing newer and better orders in them was simply an expression of what Christians understand themselves as called and enabled to do by the grace of God. And while it might have been easier to discover that by walking labyrinths or reading Hildegard of Bingen or reflecting on the world in a grain of sand, writing to a public that, for the most part, didn't share my faith was both more productive and, because it was more difficult, more rewarding. When I started the job, I wrote to express my faith. By its conclusion, I was writing to discover it. And that made the project a marvelous thing.

It wasn't always fun to wonder every week whether I'd have anything to say that might change somebody's mind. And the fact that at some point along the way I discovered I had picked up a new spiritual discipline didn't really help that much. Writing editorials, like practicing the more recognized spiritual disciplines (e. g., daily prayer, meditation, scripture reading, etc.), tends toward long stretches of tedious, boring, endlessly repetitive, and regularly frustrating activity interrupted occasionally by moments of insight, panic, fear, and joy. But it was wonderful to discover every week (well, at least some of them, anyway) that what I had to say changed me. Maybe that's why it never bothered me that I didn't write like a reporter.

The War-on-Christmas Season

(Appeared December 10, 2006)

It's happened again. We turned the calendar to December and the "War on Christmas" season began. It isn't, by the way, the Christmas season—but more on that momentarily. Whether because they're worried about Bill O'Reilly, John Gibson, and the social influence of Fox News or because they figure they'll make more money if they pander to a certain type of pallid-faithed Christian, stores like Walmart, Target, Sears, and Macy's are returning to their traditional "Merry Christmas!" greetings. Jeremiads about how writing "X-mas" takes the "Christ" out of "Christmas" start up again. And debates about nativity scenes on public property are mixed with heavy doses of collective indignation, thin theology, legal inanity, and inaccurate histories (so inaccurate one begins to doubt they could actually be the product of willful deception), and stirred.

Since all these battles have something to do with the relation of Christianity and culture, it might be helpful to view them through the lenses of the Christian faith. So as a fairly devout Christian and someone with a bit of theological training, let me lob a couple of my own grenades into the fray of inane battles during this war season. First, though, a warning: what follows may seem a bit peculiar to many readers—more sermonic than editorial. Surely, though, it's more peculiar to call for a culture war defending the place of the Christian faith therein without actually recognizing the language or vision of that faith. To do otherwise would be like carrying out arguments for English-only curricula in public schools—but only in German by those who are home-schooled. Now to grenade lobbing.

First, at least according to the long history of the Christian church, we are not in the Christmas season. That season begins not the day after Thanksgiving, the day the White House lights its tree, or any time any mall decorates itself in red and green. The Christmas season begins on Christmas day. We are in the season of Advent, which is a time of patient waiting, not frenetic activity. The Christmas season begins after Advent and continues for twelve days until Epiphany (yes, that is where the song about a partridge in a pear tree comes from).

One of the primary reasons that Americans understand the Christmas season as coming before, rather than after Christmas, is that retailers wanted it that way because that's where the money is. So last year when retailers tried to go to less religiously particular greetings and took it in the teeth (and, to believe O'Reilly and Gibson, in the bottom line) from the Fox not-quite-news folks and their fans, my admittedly petty response was, "Serves them right. Hoist them upon their own petards." At least their return to "Merry Christmas!" greetings is more transparently self-serving.

Second, if, for some reason, the retailers were actually to consult with anyone whose faith commitments and theological training ran deeper than the O'Reilly/Gibson gang, they might discover that the seemingly more innocuous "Happy Holidays" greeting of last year could be a more theologically correct thing to say to Christians than "Merry Christmas." The argument is a bit complicated, but follow me here: If Jesus is the "reason for the season" and if, as St. Paul thought, Jesus came not just to save human beings but to redeem time itself, and if redemption has something to do with making whatever is redeemed holy, and if "holiday" is actually derived from "holy day," then every day—including the ones before Christmas—is a holiday. *Ergo*, "Happy Holidays!" is always an appropriate greeting for those wishing to court Christians (or at least their wallets). Q. E. D.

Third, if the point of all these battles is to put "Christ back in Christmas" and "Christmas" back into the category of favored holiday for this "Christian nation" (I use the quotation marks intentionally; I have reservations about whether any of those things have been or ought to be the case), then I seriously doubt that the way to do it is by manipulating companies, using the media to whip people into a frenzy, or claiming that majority should rule. My suspicion is that if Christ is going to get back into Christmas, it's going to happen in the same way it did the first time: as the result of a miraculous act by a gracious God. And since the first time it happened, Jesus came preaching good news to the poor, release to the captives, the recovery of sight to the blind, and freedom for the oppressed, I'm fairly certain it's not going to look like economic extortion, mass manipulation, and vulgar democracy.

So to Bill, John, and the rest of the Christmas culture warriors who want to fight battles on behalf of all of us Christians: thanks, but no thanks. We already have a savior, and it isn't you. And until he comes again (we are in Advent after all), would you please practice enough decorum not to try to foul things up any further?

Oh—and Happy Holidays!

Tragic Theology

(Appeared April 29, 2007)

The days following tragedies like those last week in Blacksburg, Virginia are both heady and dangerous for clergy. Churches whose day-to-day work has gone ignored are suddenly loci of activity as people come to them seeking solace, companionship, and answers. Perhaps this is as it should be. Churches have long been in the business of comforting those who mourn and sitting with those who struggle with questions. These are but two of the important and underappreciated civic services that churches provide, and as both a Christian and citizen, I'm grateful they do so.

So why is it that I get so edgy as I watch interviews with clergy? Partly it's because I worry that someone will say something stupid—though more often than not, that's only because they are asked something stupid. Partly it's because I worry that they'll not be able to say something important—though more often than not, that's because they are asked something unanswerable. Mostly, though, it's because I worry that in contemporary American culture, their role in comforting those who grieve can inhibit their ability to sit with those who struggle with questions.

In 1966, Philip Rieff published *The Triumph of the Therapeutic*. In it, he argued that many forms of psychotherapy are premised on the conviction that if we work hard enough at getting our heads right, we can be okay (as in "I'm okay; you're okay"). More broadly, he suggested that these forms of psychotherapy have become a form of religious faith in Western culture—one that is too shallow and too individualistic to address the problems that persons in that culture face. Unfortunately, much that passes for pastoral care from the church turns more on Rieff's therapeutic culture than its own ecclesial one. And almost every time I see reporters interview clergy about a tragedy, I hear both the media's assumption that the church's role in such instances is to provide therapy *a la* Rieff and the cleric's affirmation that the media's assumption is correct.

When clergy get asked the question about what this all means, they tend toward one of three therapeutic and tragic responses (each of which, by the way, has an equally troubling secular manifestation):

1. The tough-love approach: "God is punishing us." (or, more likely, punishing "them," since one of our instinctive responses to disaster is to distance ourselves from it and those who suffer it). "This is the fault of Virginia Tech (and, by extension, the liberalism of higher education) for letting its students run too free." "If we'd outlaw handguns . . ." "If we allowed students to carry handguns . . ."

2. The big-picture approach: "This is all somehow a part of God's plan."—as if a little creative destruction should be no big deal in the grand scheme of things and we just need to get over our various senses of loss, grief, anger, frustration, and helplessness. "It's because Cho Seung Hui suffered from mental illness . . ."

3. The God-feels-your-pain approach: "God is suffering with us in this"—which treats the importance of connection with others not only as what we need in the face of such questions but as if it's all we need to answer them. "Virginia Tech comes together" "Churches ring their bells at noon on Friday as a sign of solidarity with those who are suffering."

What makes these answers therapeutic is that they help at least some segments of the population figure out something to do with their grief—albeit in ways that can exacerbate others' grief. What makes them tragic is that while they each contain enough truth to comfort some of us, they also carry within themselves the seeds of our undoing. The tough-love answer emphasizes the importance of recognizing that actions have implications but misses the infinitely more significant point that the God worshipped by Christians is better described in terms of love and redemption than vengeance and destruction. The big-picture answer calls us to situate tragedies in the far larger context of God's activity on earth so as not to be overwhelmed by those tragedies but misses both the existential reality of feeling overwhelmed and the pastoral sensitivity to recognize that maybe this isn't the best time to defend God's sovereignty. And while the God-feels-your-pain answer at least gets the Christian sense of divine compassion right, it gives short-shrift to the deeper Christian claim that God is doing (and has done) something about suffering.

Moreover, they all share one deeply troubling characteristic: the therapeutic conviction described by Rieff that if we can get our heads right about this tragedy, we can solve it and thereby be okay again. Though there are better and worse responses to the questions that tragedies raise, the implicit notion that theology is essentially an answer-giving enterprise not only misses the way theology works but presumes that it ought to look like psychotherapy with a spiritual veneer.

Whatever else ministers might say to those who suffer after tragedies like those in Blacksburg, they ought not fall into the trap of answer-giving as a way of resolving grief, pain, and anger. At such times, "I wish I understood" is a better response than "I think I know." The cruel pretentiousness of the claim that we can discern some larger meaning in all this is exceeded only by the statement that there is none.

Faithful Politics?

(Appeared November 25, 2007)

Televangelist Pat Robertson has endorsed Rudy Giuliani—a pro-choice candidate—for the presidency because, apparently, he thinks Giuliani has the best chance of defeating Hillary Clinton. The National Right to Life Committee has endorsed Fred Thompson—who hasn't supported the Human Life Amendment they advocate—for the presidency because, apparently, they don't like the pro-choice Giuliani and don't trust the "tell me what you want me to say" Mitt Romney. And Paul Weyrich, one of the founders of the Moral Majority, has decided to back Romney, a Mormon.

It's hard not to look at religious social conservativism and think it's lost its way. Are religious social conservatives really that reactionary? Has political expediency trumped theological principles? The answers to those two questions are probably, "Yes, they can be" and "Sadly, no" respectively.

The religious right has been reactionary almost since its inception. This is a movement, after all, that sprang to political prominence by helping a twice-married Hollywood actor who seldom darkened the door of a church defeat a

self-described born-again Christian and Sunday School teacher because they favored (and shaped) President Reagan's platform over President Carter's. Their fundamentalist theological leanings are a reaction against the way modernity shaped Christianity even though, ironically, those leanings are also founded in modernist conceptions of science, truth, and politics. Discovering that real people tend not to be as foul as they think, they react by reshaping their opponents into either the mythically monstrous (e.g., "secular humanism"—as if U.S. society has ever been secular) or treating them as far more threatening in their minds than in real life. (Seriously: is gay marriage really a bigger threat to the American family than rampant divorce?) So that folks like Robertson and Weyrich are behaving in politically reactionary ways is no surprise.

But while behaving in politically reactionary ways may make it a bit harder to see the theological vision that stimulates such reactivity, that behavior isn't inconsistent with their theological vision. That vision is based in the very kind of apocalyptic escapism that has made the *Left Behind* novels so popular: The world is evil and getting worse. Knowing this, the chosen few anticipate being raptured up out of the world of moral degradation and material suffering, but until that point will fight a kind of rear-guard action to save those they can even if that means damning those who have a different vision. Set aside the way that description of the world contradicts the church's long tradition of believing that God created the world good and, in spite of sin, has refused to give it up to darkness. Set aside the way their conviction about saving those they can contradicts the New Testament's claim that we are saved not by Christians but by Christ. Set aside the way church theologians have historically thought of hell not as the world that the raptured are leaving behind so much as those doomed for hell being pulled out—being raptured away from—the world as God transforms it. Those are all theological arguments for another day.

What is clear from the theological vision of the Robertsons and Weyriches is that if the world is foul, then politics—which is nothing more or less than the way people structure their patterns for living together in the world—is also foul. And if you think your hands are already dirty from coming into contact with politics, then your only political rule is probably to do whatever it takes to win—or to keep those you despise from winning. As such, it manages to come across as impatient (with democratic processes, with others, and ultimately with the measured movement of time itself), disappointed (with the way it believes the world is turning out), and contemptuous (of those who don't see things their way). It's not that political expediency trumped theological principles; it's that political expediency is the only available expression of these particular principles.

Thus we can trace the latest political failings of these leaders to the failings of their theological perspectives. For in spite of a wide range of opinions within the church about whether and how Christians should engage in political matters, impatience, disappointment, and contempt shouldn't drive that engagement. Indeed, it is their antitheses that should be promoted: patience in dealing with the way God works according to God's timeline rather than ours, hope that God's work is toward salvation and the transformation of the world rather than damnation and the world's destruction, and love for others—even and perhaps especially for those who are different from us.

Christians behave in lots of different ways when it comes to politics—many of them, admittedly, not especially virtuous—but the kind of political behavior now being shown by Robertson, Weyrich, and others is especially revelatory of the character of their theology. There are reasonable (though certainly not universally shared) grounds for favoring many of their political positions, including that most contentious of positions: a strict opposition to abortion. But from a Christian perspective, it is hard to find grounds for favoring their vision of political engagement. The ironies apparent in the way they've rallied behind the current presidential candidates only highlight the deficiency of that vision.

Easter and the End of Culture Wars
(Appeared April 8, 2007)

Christians around the world are gathering for Easter today, celebrating the resurrection of Jesus of Nazareth. At least to judge from swelling church attendance, fancy brunches in restaurants, an abundance of women's hats, and a general feeling of springtime friendliness on the part of folks everywhere, nearly everybody nods pleasantly toward Christianity today. Because today is Easter and Easter continues to exert such a pull not only on the Christian church but upon larger society, today is also a day on which I will make the Christian viewpoint from which I always write more explicit than normal. Call it Easter license.

Easter is the most important day in the Christian year. And, like all truly important things, it is among the least understood—as much Christian behavior on the other 364 days of the year would so suggest. My primary piece of evidence that Christians do not understand Easter is that even after the resurrection, we continue to behave in politically inappropriate ways. And the foremost evidence of inappropriate political behavior is our willingness to instigate and engage in culture wars.

A (rather dense) bit of background: in 1991, James Davison Hunter published *Culture Wars: The Struggle to Define America*. He argued that American society is undergoing a series of profound conflicts—a sort of war—being fought over which system of symbols will be used by American society to understand itself. Each of these symbol-systems is manifested in and defended by powerful institutions like religious bodies, educational organizations, media services, legal entities, and political associations. Whoever gets to dictate the symbols by which society understands itself gets to direct culture—and for those in the war it's vitally important that culture be directed in the "right" way for the good of everyone in society. The winners of the culture wars not only dictate a society's vision of the world, they win in such a way that their vision becomes tantamount to common sense.

U.S. Christians are in the thick of this war. Whether battling what we perceive to be immoral sexual practices, unsustainable visions of the family, unjust economic arrangements, or idolatrous political systems, Christians on both the left and the right have routinely advanced the argument that we must either create or recover a "Christian culture" on which to found a good and just society. And toward that end, we've been willing to behave in execrable ways, including running "covert" candidates for local political bodies, emphasizing wedge issues like gay marriage during elections, threatening the doctors and staff of abortion clinics, and demonizing those with whom we disagree. Indeed, Christians sometimes seem especially fearful of losing the culture wars and have therefore been especially willing to behave in ways that look almost nothing like the vision of behavior that Jesus laid out in the Sermon on the Mount.

That we behave badly is unsurprising. One of the central premises of Christianity, after all, is that everyone—whether Christian or not—will behave badly and is powerless to correct that behavior through their own efforts. Still, that we behave badly in this way is not only disturbing but a fairly clear instance of "we should know better." The reason we should know better—to return to the Easter theme—is that belief in Jesus' resurrection all-but-compels it.

When we Christians claim that Jesus' resurrection has changed things, we ought to mean at least the following: First, that in the resurrection, God has ultimately defeated everything that would stand between God's creation and its final redemption. And, second, that Jesus' resurrection inaugurates but does not complete that final redemption and that until God brings about that final redemption, we cannot look at any victory in any setting as final and complete.

In the context of Christian engagement with culture, then, the first expression of the claim that Jesus' resurrection has changed things ought to include the recognition that there is no war that we still need to fight. The war is already over; God has already triumphed. So marching as to war isn't an act of faith so much as a kind of faithlessness—a refusal to accept the good news of the faith. Christians seeking war are actually engaged in a kind of spiritual suicide.

And the second expression of that claim recognizes that though the war is over, the "mopping up" isn't—and will not be finished until God brings about the Kingdom of God in all its fullness. Until then, though, attempts to force culture to conform to a single particular vision of that Kingdom are not only premature; they are doomed to failure. This side of eternity, there will continue to be injustice, mercilessness, and wars (including of the cultural variety). And because they continue, Christians ought to continue to work for justice, mercy, and peace—to align ourselves with the work that God is doing. But because of the resurrection, that work is based neither on a heroic stand against the dark forces of culture nor an idolatrous claim that we Christians can defeat those forces. It is based on hope and expressed in the patient work that comes with waiting for God to finish what God has started. Whatever else they are, the culture wars are neither hopeful nor patient—and those who believe in the resurrection should stop fighting them.

A Job for Today

(Appeared September 30, 2007)

Earlier this month, a Nebraska state senator filed a lawsuit against God. That's not especially odd. Atypical perhaps, but not odd. The long histories of both Judaism and Christianity include repeated attempts to put God on trial. Many of the Psalms—not to mention the book of Job, which continues to be one of the profoundest investigations into justice, righteousness, and the occurrence of wrongdoing ever written—do the same. And what would Christianity be without the trial of "the Word made flesh" at its center? There is an entire history of great and not-so-great literature that tries God, including novels like *The Brothers Karamozov* by Dostoevsky, plays like "J. B." by Pulitzer Prizewinning poet Archibald MacLeish and essays like "God in the Dock" by Christian apologist C. S. Lewis. And how often have many of us, in the face of personal or international disasters, felt deserving of a few answers from the Almighty?

The Nebraska senator in question is Ernie Chambers. That's neither odd nor surprising. Chambers has made a reputation for himself as a maverick, an outspoken agnostic,

and an attention-seeker. As those who know of him would expect, the lawsuit is rich in clever, if smug, language-play: since the defendant is omnipresent, he must be in Douglas County as well and, therefore, within that county's jurisdiction; since he's also omniscient, the court should waive personal service to notify the defendant; it would be "a futile and perhaps unlawful act to nail a notice to the front door" of each of the defendant's agents (or at least in bad taste to do so to Lutheran doors); the defendant has caused "fearsome floods, egregious earthquakes, horrendous hurricanes, terrifying tornadoes, pestilential plagues, ferocious famines, devastating drouths [sic] . . ." (Plantiff earns an "A" in alliteration, if not insight). Suing God sounds just about right for Chambers.

Chambers' point in filing the suit was to make a point about frivolous lawsuits by arguing that the law, at least as it stands in Nebraska, allows anyone to sue anyone over anything. Using a lawsuit against God to make that point isn't that odd. Ineffective and ironic perhaps, but not that odd. The need for torte reform is widely agreed upon even if the methods for pursuing that reform are not. So while we might raise questions about taking a much honored approach to dealing with important questions of human existence and turning it into the occasion to do some finger-shaking at a weak point in contemporary jurisprudence, we shouldn't see it as odd in a culture that regularly transforms the profound into the banal and provocative questions into popular ones.

Miraculously, two court filings from the defendant appeared—*as if from nowhere!*—at the Douglas County District Courthouse. That's not especially odd. Impious and more than a little goofy, perhaps, but not odd. God's defenders have always been more than willing to leap to his defense and regularly do so by claiming either to have a divine mandate from him or to actually be him. (One wonders who has bigger *cojones*: someone suing God or someone pretending to be God in response?) The filings claim that God is immune from earthly laws and that the Douglas County Courthouse lacks jurisdiction. They also list "St. Michael the Archangel" as a witness. Where, exactly, would that witness sit in the courtroom?

It's not even odd that the news services and blogs would pick up on this story and publicize it. Hackneyed, perhaps, but not odd. In the interest of "the public's right to know" and the chattering class's right to e-hash their religious sentiments of the moment, such a news story is almost certain to get more attention than it deserves. Nothing like a slow news day to give an excuse for further domesticating the transcendent.

What is odd, however, is that "God's" filings also give an argument in defense of "fearsome floods, egregious earthquakes," etc: the gift of free will to human beings. "I created man and woman with free will and next to the promise of immortal life, free will is my greatest gift to you," one filing reads. Setting aside the fact that there's a difference between "immortal life" and "eternal life," it's more than a little peculiar that anyone would think that human free will has been the cause of all the world's natural disasters. I'm as conscious as Al Gore is that human beings are having an effect on the environment. But is this really what we've been reduced to: playing the "free will" card every time we confront tragedy, no matter how abstractly or juridically? That's not an answer; it's an excuse to avoid asking the questions.

And while I'm happy to concede that this petty little exchange between Senator Chambers and "God" is hardly representative of the depth with which many people continue to struggle with difficult questions, that this case ever got any attention is its own sad sign of the shrunken standards we use as springboards for stimulating speech. (How's that for alliteration, Senator?) I'd rather talk with Ivan Karamozov.

An Elegy for the Daily Paper

(Accessed November 26, 2006)

The day after I agreed to write a weekly editorial for *The Sunday Paper*, I received my weekly issue of *The Economist*. Its cover story was entitled "Who Killed the Newspaper?"

This was not a good omen. Depending on how you think of *The Sunday Paper*, I'm either joining in a dying enterprise or helping to hasten its death—I'm either doomed or cruel.

The *Economist* article cited statistics on the loss of readership and revenue by newspapers over the past ten years. It recited an unsurprising litany of reasons for those losses: access to news-for-free sources (like the paper you, dear reader, are holding in the hand that doesn't have a cup of overpriced coffee in it); the growth of the internet; changes in public taste; resistance to change in the newspaper industry.

In the face of the "death" of daily newspapers, it's no wonder that free weeklies like *The Sunday Paper* are reproducing like origami bunnies: in-your-face covers, attention to local events (especially odd ones), titillating pictures advertising various bodily augmentations and the various garments you can wear post-surgery, words you can't say in front of your five-year old—and all for free! The free papers, at least, know what sells.

I'm sure all these moribund daily newspapers can learn something from the free weeklies, online news sources, or even journals like *The Economist*. But I don't see that they can overcome the thing that most distinguishes them from other sources of news and entertainment; namely, that daily newspapers are boring.

I have reached this rather anecdotal conclusion by watching what my own family does with our daily newspaper. Generally, my wife quickly scans it to see if there is anything she needs to be aware of. I skim the front page and then jump to the editorial page. And our daughter, like kids everywhere, goes straight to the comics. Collectively, we're looking for anything with a pulse.

It's no wonder newspapers are trying to reinvigorate themselves with new formats, revised special weekly sections, shorter articles, flashier graphics, and online editions (the risk here being that they're putting makeup on a corpse rather than reanimating a body).

But I worry that in trying to reinvigorate themselves, daily newspapers may be losing one of their most important qualities: that they *are* boring. It seems to me that one of the great strengths of daily newspapers has been their willingness to bring not only the big front-page stuff to us, but the remote, the wonkish, and the quotidian as well. Life, they remind us, is about more than major events, glamorous celebrities, and a bit of mostly innocent voyeurism.

Nowhere is this more the case than in liberal democracies, which as political manifestations are centered in the mundane. They emphasize politics writ small (school board meetings, voting in primaries, petitioning local representatives about speed bumps and stop signs) in order to train citizens in the types of civic virtues that can resist passivity and apathy on the one side and provincialism and ideological fervor on the other. Where there is an independent press (or at least a press that seeks to be independent), newspapers are democracy's response to those who would insist that everyone either share a common vision and speak the same language or step aside and keep silent. They are liberal democracy's preventive medicine for the ailments of procrustean politics.

Attention to the mundane may kill newspapers, but I suspect that it helps keep liberal democracies alive. If, in a (hopefully) distant future, a history of the failure of American democracy ever gets written, it may look back to the death of newspapers and see a cause: that we sacrificed involvement for entertainment, boredom for brevity, and the intractable untidiness of the everyday for the easy answers of ideologies. And if *The Economist* is right and newspapers are dead, then shouldn't those of us who value liberal democracy at least be looking for something as boring as they are to replace them?

So, to those of you who have come this far in the article: Thank you for reading. Really. We'll be here for you every week. But would it kill you to buy a newspaper?

Q&A

(Appeared January 20, 2008)

Question: What country has the following ten characteristics?

1. Its pre-history fascinates archaeologists, who have unearthed amazing discoveries from it over the past several decades.

2. It is the most stable and prosperous country in its area of the world.

3. It has a history of democracy though surrounded by a number of undemocratic neighbor states.

4. Its pro-Western stance is not shared by many of its neighbors.

5. Many of its neighbors have been subject to national unrest and chaos over the past decade. As a result, it struggles to deal with refugees.

6. In the recent past, the U.S. sent a significant number of troops to one neighboring country in a military endeavor that many people consider a failure; currently, the U.S. is being asked to consider sending troops to another of its neighboring countries.

7. It has dealt with significant acts of terrorism over the past dozen years, including bombings by Al Qaeda.

8. It is a popular site for western tourism in spite of the instability of some of its neighboring countries and the internal threats of violence.

9. While it is has a long coast, these tourists tend not to come to visit its shores. Instead, their interests tend to be further inland.

10. It receives substantial aid from the United States.

Answer: It's a trick question because there are two solutions to it. The first and more obvious is Israel. The second is Kenya. Now, I should be clear: Israel and Kenya are very different places—and not only geographically. They have different roles in the geopolitical world, different strengths and needs, and significantly different relations with the U.S. But perhaps those ten similarities might suggest we pause long enough to think about the U.S. relationship with Kenya even as President Bush makes his trip through the Middle East.

Question: What's going on in Kenya worth pausing about?

Answer: A botched—and possibly rigged—election at the end of December was the catalyst for rioting that led to the deaths of up to a thousand people, renewed tribal conflicts after a long period of peace, and the displacement of up to half a million people trying to escape the violence. Nobel Prize winner Desmond Tutu and the presidents of three African nations—including John Kufuor of Ghana, who is the current chairman of the African Union—have all attempted to get the leaders of the two opposing political parties to negotiate an amicable way to settle the conflict but have met with little success. In a country of roughly 35 million people, almost everybody has been touched somehow by these events. Emails I've received from friends, students, and colleagues in churches across Kenya repeat the same refrain: we're being stretched beyond our limits in our ability to welcome people fleeing violence. If this situation isn't solved soon and unless we get substantial help, the prospects for national stability look bleak. Of course, unless you were reading my emails or the below-the-fold articles in the middle of the "World" section of the newspaper, you probably didn't hear much about Kenya.

Question: Why should we care?

Answer: This is one of those wonderful occasions when what is right to do, what is advantageous to do, and what is possible to do all converge. We should care about what's going on in Kenya because we should care about any situation in which persons' lives are suddenly destabilized by the need to flee. Compassion simply ought to be what we do, and while we might debate the best way to express that compassion, it's hard to imagine anyone getting much moral traction out of the idea that loving our neighbors is an idea we can just ignore. We should care about what's going on in Kenya because the possibility of another failed or conflicted state in Africa is bad for American interests. For years, foreign affairs experts have been warning us of the dangers of such parts of Africa turning into new havens for recruiting and training terrorists, new points of origin for global pandemics, new sources of drugs and weapons, and therefore new money-sinks for increasingly mandatory Western aid. Kenya probably wouldn't fall to the level of neighbors like Somalia or Sudan, but Kenya's fall will certainly make dealing with such neighbors far more difficult. And we should care because Kenya's history of comparative stability makes it far more likely that attention right now can return it to political (and economic and tribal) stability soon.

Question: What can we do?

Answer: If you are a person of faith, find out what your religious community and its sister institutions can do; odds are good that they are already doing something. Write your congressional representatives and request that they pay attention to Kenya as well. And in the middle of reading about Britney Spears' crisis, Tony Romo's girlfriend, or Hillary Clinton's tears, pay attention to the below-the-fold articles in the middle of the newspaper.

Saying Something Important

(Appeared June 3, 2007)

Until the day before I wrote this, I had intended to write Something Important about American culture or politics. Then I saw Spiderman 3. As a topic, Spidey 3 may not have the *gravitas* of other topics, but I figure a movie with the highest grossing opening weekend ever probably deserves some attention on the cultural front. Besides: I just finished a three-week series that set a new bar for levels of abstraction, so maybe you, dear reader, are ready for a change. I know I am. Normally, I would warn readers that haven't seen the movie that they may want to stop reading now but at this point, who hasn't seen the movie???

As you read forward, keep in mind: I liked Spidey 1 and 2. As for 3, my review can be summarized in three words: soppy, sloppy, and schlocky. To wit:

Soppy. There are more misty eyes and tearful moments in this movie—at least for the characters though not so much for the audience—than any three chick-flicks. And they aren't brief moments. They're long, drawn out, "camera gazing soulfully into the eyes of soulfully-gazing characters" mo-

ments. Even a *man made of sand* cries. I didn't put a stopwatch to it, but I'd guess the amount of time we spend looking at eyes swelling with tears may be greater than the amount of time we spend watching CGI action sequences. All movies are manipulative; this one is embarrassingly so. In Harry Osborne, the filmmakers actually give us a character we're supposed to feel a bit of sympathy for, then think of as evil, then like, then dislike again, then like, and then—again, only with more fervor—feel sympathy for. It's all rather whiplashy. Likewise—and without any reason so substantive as Harry's nasty bump on the head—we're supposed to go back and forth about Sandman/Flint Marko, who the writers, in one of the more transparently manipulative moves I can remember in movie history, actually ask us to accept as the guy who really killed Uncle Ben. I can only guess that the most difficult aspect of acting for this movie was getting used to the fresh-cut onions they must have hidden all over the set. This is clearly a movie that wants its audience to feel.

Sloppy. Even setting aside the character miscues—like the fact that Spidey has apparently traded in his spider sense (which never kicks in, no matter the danger) for the ability to play a mean piano or the sword that's supposed to be really significant for Harry-the-Goblin (only he almost never uses it)—the movie, though it wants us to think, thinks, itself, in sloppy ways. Spidey 3, like its predecessors, is about identity: good side/bad side, successful/failure, ego/alter-ego. To make sure we don't miss this point, just about everybody in the movie gets doubled here: good Peter Parker/bad Peter Parker, good Harry/bad Harry, Peter Parker/Eddie Brock, Spiderman/Venom, Mary Jane Watson/Gwen Stacy, etc. And the point of all this reflection on identity? Are we supposed to think about our own darker and lighter angels? About the dangers of power? About the struggles that superheroes must go through? About the fluidity of identity in a postmodern world? Beats me. No thoughts are developed in a sufficiently substantial way to warrant our reflection. They're replaced by special effects and a storyline (though not a plotline) that pushes us from emotional moment to emotional moment. As a result, ideas about identity that are intended to be provocative end up diffused, defeated, or, worse, practically drooling in their stupidity. Maybe the director's cut will add all the scenes back in that are now on the editing

floor. Probably, though, it will just repeat the schlocky moral of the story.

Schlocky. The moral of the story—and it does have one in the most obvious and not-especially-thoughtful of ways—is that we need to judge less and forgive more because things are more morally complex than they sometimes seem. So in the end, Harry Osborne forgives Peter Parker for killing his dad, Mary Jane forgives him for being a self-absorbed twit, and Peter forgives Flint Marko for (accidentally, it turns out) killing Uncle Ben. Now, I'm all for emphasizing forgiveness. I think forgiveness is necessary for healthy internal and interpersonal relationships and perhaps even more important for sustaining social and political relations. And it's certainly central to Christian ethics. But the movie treats forgiveness in morally simplistic ways and such moral simplicity—especially when it comes packaged in emotional soppiness—isn't a virtue; it's a vice wearing a smiley-face button. When Peter forgives Marko for killing Uncle Ben and then lets him go—ignoring the fact that Marko has done tremendous damage to the city and, we have to imagine, to many of its inhabitants—we shouldn't be morally gratified. We should be disturbed at such a self-absorbed vision of forgiveness and its benefits. If superheroes fight for justice, shouldn't we at least be encouraged to wonder what justice looks like here???

There's no reason to expect much from summer blockbusters beyond a little excitement, a laugh or two, and a chance to escape. But Spiderman 3 seems to want to say Something Important about feelings and ideas and morality—at least until its CGI-enhanced version of ADHD kicks in and, instead, anesthetizes us. Which, come to think of it, sounds a lot like what is going on in American culture and politics.

Oh, Happy Day?
(Appeared October 7, 2007)

Last spring, Harvard professor of psychology, language, and cognitive science Steven Pinker published his article "A History of Violence" in *The New Republic*. In it, Pinker argued that the human attraction to violence has been diminishing significantly over the past few centuries. As a species, he claimed, we're less cruel to animals, less accepting of slavery, more appalled by genocide, torture, and acts of depravity (and so on) than we were a brief hundred and fifty years ago. And while our attractions to violent games, sports, and movies may suggest a willingness to fantasize about violence, they don't necessarily seem to induce a general willingness to act on those fantasies. "The decline of violence," Pinker wrote, "is a fractal phenomenon, visible at the scale of millennia, centuries, decades, and years. It applies over several orders of magnitude of violence . . . and it appears to be a worldwide trend, though not a homogenous one" (*The New Republic Online; March 20, 2007*).

And this year, Cornell Paperbacks republished John Mueller's 2004 book *The Remnants of War* with a new preface. In that book, Mueller argued that organized and disciplined warfare between nations is becoming obsolete and has been doing so since the end of the nineteenth century.

The reason for its impending obsolescence, Mueller suggests, is that antiwar sentiment and activism have taken hold in societies around the world. The wars that remain are, by and large, criminal activities pursued by thugs for the perverse purposes of pleasure and profit.

As you look around at genocide in Darfur, barely controlled chaos in Iraq, belligerence in Iran so great that even France (France!) is talking tough, child soldiers in Uganda, a surging sex-slave trade in parts of Asia, North Korean nukes, student rampages in Blacksburg, Virginia, execution-style murders in Newark, slaughterhouse practices that would silence Upton Sinclair, dog fighting in Georgia . . . , you must have read those first two paragraphs and asked, "What in the Sam Hill is going on here???" Having read both the article and Mueller's book, I did.

But both authors make strong cases for their positions, supporting them with substantial statistics and generous anecdotal evidence. So let's suppose, just for the sake of argument, that there is something

to these claims. If so, wouldn't two questions follow: Why is this so? And, if it is so, why are so many of us tucked into existential fetal positions, curved inwards upon ourselves out of fear and self-protection in the face of the cold hard world?

Toward answering the first question, Pinker suggests four theories to answer the question of why we're getting nicer (namely, that reduced violence is the product of modernity's creation of anti-violent political systems like democracy; that increased longevity brought on by technological and economic change inhibits our willingness to think of life as cheap; that non-zero-sum games which emphasize cooperation are preferable in modern contexts but take a long time to develop; and that empathy gives an evolutionary advantage to those in large societies), each of which only pushes back the question a step: where did such political, technological, economic, and community-affirming systems come from? And from there, we're pretty quickly into metaphysical deep water. So deep, in fact, that by the end, Pinker ceases the search for causes and gives into an "I don't know why, but isn't it a good thing that it's going on" conclusion. Comforting, maybe, but hardly satisfying—especially in the face of the levels of *über*-violence we so regularly see—and certainly not likely to give us insight into the second question.

Mueller is more instructive. Wars may be diminishing as states increasingly move away from the belief that power comes only at the tip of the sword, but as the remaining wars are increasingly driven by warlords, thugs, and criminals intent not on national good but personal advantage, they are fought more cruelly. So it isn't just that those of us who look at the world from relative privilege may see horrors as more horrible because of their contrast to our comfort. It's also that the civilizing process, itself, has the ironic effect of making cruelty more cruel—and what's true in war is no less so in other situations of cruelty. As St. Augustine would remind us, since evil is always parasitic on goodness, the greater the range of goodness, the more resources there are to nourish evil.

Moreover, from our existential fetal positions, our visions of the world as worse than it actually is has the effect of tucking us in tighter on ourselves, privatizing the impact of cruelty upon our senses and further isolating us from others at the very point we may most need to be in touch with them. It's no wonder

we're attracted to the recent spate of vengeance movies: they play not only on our overweening fear but our heightened sense of isolation.

Are Pinker and Mueller right? There are certainly arguments against them. But unless we're willing to unclench just a bit, we may never get ourselves into a position to sort through the questions that Pinker or Mueller are asking, nor the questions we should ask of their answers. Which would be a shame: we could use the good news.

When the Problem is the Problem

(Appeared October 14, 2007)

An empire attempting to maintain international control and credibility in the face of upstart nations seemingly intent on undermining its power. Clashing civilizations shaped by different and seemingly incompatible religious traditions. One of those religious traditions splintering into factions intent on persecuting each other. Seemingly endless wars shaping the political sensibility of persons around the world. Political leaders seeking a way out of these messes but not agreeing with each other on what that way should be. Sound familiar? It should—if you remember your European history or you're very, very, *very* old. The events in question happened in the seventeenth century and led to the Peace of Westphalia, which ended both the Thirty Years' War and the Eighty Years' War in Europe and settled a series of conflicts between the waning Holy Roman Empire and a collection of upstart nation-states intent on pursuing their own political and religious paths.

Contrary to conventional wisdom, history never repeats itself: this simply isn't seventeenth-century Europe. History does, however,

regularly riff on its past: the way we think in the present is shaped by the ways we've thought in the past. That, in itself, isn't problematic. Contexts are never quite the same but the wisdom of an earlier time is both vital and inevitable in thinking about the problems of the present day. After all, we all stand on the shoulders of our intellectual forbearers. So unless we are willing to abandon our minds and surrender our footing, we will use what we have learned—and therein, who we have become—to better move forward through time.

The catch, though, is that yesterday's answers were imperfect then and don't entirely fit now. The chief flaw of the Peace of Westphalia was that it perceived European conflicts almost exclusively as the product of religious differences between Protestants and Catholics and, as a result, advanced the idea that the best way to keep the peace was to limit the sway of religion on politics. There have been two major problems with this conclusion. First, religious convictions are neither easily contained nor inevitably likely to promote violence. And, second, it simply wasn't the case that the conflicts then were driven by religious differences. As historians have pointed out, the so-called religious wars of Europe often saw Catholics and Protestants fighting together against other Catholics and Protestants. Indeed, these historians suggest, the wars of seventeenth-century Europe and the peace that followed had far more to do with the rise of modern nation-states and their battles against earlier forms of political order. Yet conventional wisdom still holds that the wars were about religion and the solution was to contain it.

Today, we hear much about the failures of Iraqi government to produce a stable armistice between Shia and Sunni religious factions intent on their exclusivist projects of power-mongering and retribution. It is as if the power of religion will be the ultimate cause of Iraq's eventual undoing. Regardless of their disagreements, both Democrats and Republicans seemingly agree that the problem with Iraq is, increasingly, religious in shape and that, therefore, the solution will have to be a kind of stability made possible via acceptance of ethnic pluralism and religious quietude.

Shia and Sunni factions have certainly played a major role in contributing to Iraq's instability. The patterns of vengeance-seeking and religio-ethnic division are clearly pronounced and deeply troubling.

But before we jump to a "Peace of Westphalia" conclusion, we should note the existence of considerable evidence that undermines that conclusion. First, prior to the U.S. invasion, Shiites and Sunnis lived—well, if not *comfortably* together, at least in far more amicable relations than today. And while this may partly have been because of the repressive regime that Saddam had in place, that Sunni-dominant government can't explain the degree of Sunni-Shiite intermarriage and shared communities in Iraq's urban centers. Second, in many places in Iraq, conflict hasn't broken down along Sunni/Shia lines. For example, in southern Iraq, Shiites fight each other and in central Iraq, Sunnis side with the U.S. against other Sunni groups.

And, third, while religious convictions can have a profound formative influence on the perspectives and actions of individuals and small groups, history suggests that they are comparatively weak in driving institutional structures—which means that trying to order Iraqi politics by ordering Iraqi faiths is likely to be not only politically unfeasible but imprudent as well.

I have long argued that we need to pay attention to religious convictions when addressing political issues, so I will be the first to emphasize the impact of religion on political thought. But we shouldn't overestimate its impact such that we can no longer accurately identify or address its actual expression. As long, though, as we see religion as a driving problem in Iraq, we're going to have a problem with our problem.

3 Public Engagement and Christian Hope

Writing a weekly editorial column can be an excuse to take a good habit and turn it into an addiction. The good habit is keeping an eye on the news and attending to the thoughts of those who are analyzing it. The addiction is being a political junkie. While I was writing, I read two major daily newspapers, *The Economist, The New Republic, The Atlantic, The Christian Century, Foreign Affairs,* and *The New York Review of Books* habitually. I made frequent forays into both left-leaning (*The New Yorker, Harper's Magazine, Mother Jones*) and right-leaning (*The Weekly Standard, The American Spectator, The National Review*) journals. I'd repress my gag reflex and watch CNN or Fox News on TV while working out at the gym. I even tried to convince myself that staying up late to watch *The Daily Show with Jon Stewart* and *The Colbert Report* was a professional responsibility instead of a guilty pleasure.

Part of the addiction had to do with trolling through the news to see where interesting stories might be coming from—even if the stories, themselves, were minor. Why else would I devote a column to the Bush Administration's nomination of James Holsinger as Surgeon General?* Part of the addiction had to do with finding those analyses of current events that could teach me something important. And mostly it had to do with the fear that I'd write something either stupid or—almost worse— unoriginal. Seeking the next score; looking for better product; fearing what would happen if I couldn't get something worthwhile: there's a reason they'd call people like me junkies. (To tighten the analogy still further, when I stopped writing weekly columns I had to go cold turkey on the news and analysis for a month or two. And after that, I didn't even want to be around the news for quite a while; newspapers would go straight from the driveway to the recycle bin. I did keep watching Stewart and Colbert, though. Call them political methadone for a recovering news junkie.)

One of the things that became transparently clear to me while I was doing all that reading and writing my editorials is that politics is, increasingly, a spectator sport.

That's not the same thing as saying that politics doesn't really matter to us. It does matter. A lot. But for many of us, it seems to matter in the same way that being a Denver Broncos fan matters to me. I rejoice in their victories and die a little when they lose. I can name most of the players on the '77 Super Bowl team even though I was ten years old at the time and it's been over thirty years since that game. I think that they should still play at Mile High Stadium, that contested calls should always go their direction, and that Randy Gradishar should be in the Hall of Fame. I forgive their players when they get flagged for illegal behavior though I am outraged when the same fouls are committed by players on other teams (especially the Oakland Raiders, who are, of course, the collective antithesis of all that is good and noble). After John Elway retired, I tried cheering for other teams for a little while, but I couldn't do it.

If I'd grown up rooting for the Pittsburg Steelers—or, perhaps worse, if the Broncos had moved to another city—I'm not sure my life would have changed that dramatically. I've met a fair number of Steelers fans who are every bit as passionate about the yellow and black as I am about the orange and blue and, for the most part, they seem pretty decent (albeit confused) people. Maybe someday I'll fall for another team. But I doubt it. After so many years and so much devotion, being a Denver Broncos fan is part of who I am.

But I'm only a fan. I'm a spectator. I don't don the uniform or draw a check. I know none of the players or staff personally and they're not really out there playing for me. I get to watch. To cheer. To daydream about what it would be like to put on the pads. To enjoy (and suffer) a connection that has, over time, become quasi-mystical. But my day-to-day life doesn't turn on the team because it can't. There are other sports, other obligations, and other joys. Between draft day and training camp, I seldom give them a first thought, let alone a second one.

That's what I mean by politics being a spectator sport. We may not only watch the news to get our political fix but we'll choose which news to watch based on our political affiliation. We watch election coverage like watching play-by-play; we prefer the color commentators giving us insight into the electoral horserace more than we want them helping us make sense of the candidates' policy proposals. We trade doctored stats and stories on the players over the internet, vote the party ticket in the polling booth, forgive the (always exceptional) indiscretions of our side, and club the other side with theirs because that's how they always behave. We treat elected officials more like celebrities than professional bureaucrats. We esteem leadership, not wonkishness. We cheer when our team wins and forecast dire consequences when the other guys do.

Perhaps spectatorial politics isn't entirely a bad thing. Its very existence may signal the levels of freedom, luxury, and leisure we live in: we can be spectators because the U.S.'s political stability and economic might means the quality of our own lives doesn't actually turn on what happens in most of the issues about which we cheer. A corrupted form of political engagement still beats being unable to engage because there aren't any viable choices for us to make or our lives are threatened for making such choices. Neither, though, is it an especially good thing since it leaves us ill-equipped to discriminate between candidates and issues and unpracticed at thinking for ourselves.

Again: it's not that we think politics doesn't matter. We think it matters a lot. We're just not sure how most of what passes for politics matters in our day-to-day lives and so when faced with political decisions we have trouble telling which decisions matter a lot, which don't, and why. And, worse, we seem to be having more and more trouble getting along with the fans of the other teams. It's not that we ignore politics; to judge from the preponderance of cable news and internet blogs, we may pay too much attention to politics. It's that we've done little to train ourselves to see politics differently.

Among the two chief bits of evidence for this are, first, that we increasingly treat all politics as partisan and, second, that we increasingly treat partisanship as a problem. Partisanship may not be the problem, though. Maybe the problem is with a vision of politically engaged citizens as always partisan and a vision of partisanship as foul. Such visions force a false choice: either pure but passive or polluted but powerful. In accepting that false choice, we reinforce its corrupt consequences. To get out of such a predicament, though, means revising both our vision of politics and our judgments about partisanship. In part that means that rather than rejecting partisanship, we might do better to recognize its benefits while also seeing ourselves and each other as greater than the sum of our partisan opinions—a point I tried to make in "Two Cheers for Partisanship."*

Of late, it seems like religion is getting dragged in as a possible cure for the problems of partisanship. Not always, of course: sometimes attention to religious perspectives is just the occasion to throw more fodder to the beast of spectatorial politics: "He goes to which church?" "She met with which cleric?" "All persons of faith should hold which political position?" Often, though, religion is treated as a cure to some of the ills of partisanship. It is supposed to provide a stabilizing influence over the whizzing to-and-fro of political gamesmanship; a sense of solemnity to counteract political bombast; a vision for the common good that can unite fans on all sides. Indeed, calls to revitalize the public sphere—to move beyond being spectators to being informed participants—often emphasize the role that religious institutions can play in shaping responsible citizens.

One of the reasons that religion is so honored is related to something Patrick Henry (of "give me liberty or give me death" fame) supposedly once said: that "[b]ad men cannot make good citizens. It is when a people forget God that tyrants forge their chains." Setting aside the debate among historians as to whether he actually said such a thing, the point is clear: religious faith prevents tyranny, whether it is the tyranny of a king or the tyranny of the mob. Some conservatives emphasize the role that religion used to play in keeping the country together (such nostalgia conveniently forgetting how good religion has been at tearing the country apart—including during the high pieties of the Civil War) and call for a return to the supposedly lost Judeo-Christian center of American morality. Some liberals emphasize the role that religion might still play in bringing the country together (such optimism nicely forgetting that very little religious thought about the future treats national stability as worth our attention) and call for churches to take up the work of transforming the nation.

Call this approach the Patrick Henry temptation. It is a temptation to believers because it is both attractive and wrong. It is attractive because it casts both church and state into their socially accepted roles: church as aid-society and state as powerful but corrupted; religion as fulfilling and politics as necessary but lacking morality; the Christian faith as salvific and the culture as in need of salvation; believers as upstanding members of society and everyone else as . . . well—what? Socially unmoored? Self-absorbed? Tossed about by the fickle waves of faddish culture?

The temptation is wrong, though, for myriad reasons. Setting aside the historical problems (the Founding Fathers were hardly of one mind on religion), the moral problems (religious people hardly have a monopoly on morality), and the cultural problems (we live in one of the most religiously diverse cultures in all of human history), there are important theological reasons that the Patrick Henry temptation is wrong and the stereotypes it reinforces (like those in the preceding paragraph) are damaging. Fortunately, because it is a temptation rather than our social fate, we can resist it.

It is those theological problems with the Patrick Henry temptation that I want to draw out. To do so, I want to ask a rather peculiar question: Does the church need the state? Since the Patrick Henry temptation assumes that the state needs the church, asking the reverse question might not only expose some of the flaws with the temptation but might help us think more constructively about how Christians ought to get involved in the public sphere in the first place. Because while engaging the state and getting involved in the public sphere are certainly not the same thing, their interests—at least in modern constitutional democracies—overlap.

Beginning with the question, "Does the church need the state?" changes the conversation. It helps the church avoid either the appearance of defensive stridency ("But you need us!") or the arrogance of triumphalist confidence ("See—you need us!"). Moreover, since it is a little-asked question, we're less likely to carry as many assumptions into the conversation. That will allow us to begin with cleaner conceptual slates and greater willingness to try some fresh theological thinking—which could, in turn, allow us to return to the more familiar question about how the state needs the church in fresh ways.

Before moving forward, though, three opening caveats are warranted. First, just as thinking about the public sphere is different than thinking about politics, so thinking about politics is not the same thing as thinking about the state. Just as there are many public matters that are not overtly political concerns, so there are many political contexts and activities that have little if anything to do with the state (think, for example, of the contexts of churches or private schools or the activities of writing letters to the editor or volunteering in civic organizations). I have elided the differences between the public generally and politics specifically by shaping a definition of politics that can encompass all interactions between people. It's a cheat, but one that works pretty well in most instances. Likewise, I have focused on the state because at least since the 1600s, the modern state has been the dominant player in all matters political and, as a result, we tend to connect the way we understand politics working to the way we understand the state. Again, it's a cheat, but one that works pretty well in most instances. I leave it to the reader to do whatever translation work is necessary to move from the descriptions of the state that follow to an understanding of politics more generally (and from the overtly political to the generally public). I figure if readers have made it this far into the book, the odds are good that they can make those translations.

The second caveat is this: according to the church's own understanding of itself, the church (and the rest of creation, for that matter) ultimately exists only by the grace of God. As such, the church doesn't *need* the state for its continued existence. The church has existed in many forms and in many states throughout its history and it still flourishes around the world. Theologically, then, the church's continued existence is contingent on the work of God, not the vagaries of history or the whims of the state.

Finally, the third caveat is that the church believes that ultimately the state as we know or imagine it has a determinate shelf life—an expiration date, if you will. At some point, states will cease to exist. That sounds ominous until you remember that the church can say something quite similar about itself: that the church as we know and imagine it will also cease to exist. In their collective place will be the New Jerusalem, the Holy City, simultaneously the full communion of all the saints (which is what the earthly church is being transformed into) and the Kingdom of God (which is what the earthly state is being transformed into). St. Augustine reminds us that the state is a failed church, a community of people brought together under common bonds attempting to live out their individual and collective divine callings. He might also have reminded us, though, that the visible church is also a failed church (albeit one that, unlike the state, recognizes that it is not yet what it will be transformed into and so is, in principle, receptive to seeing the grace of God in a way that the state is not). So while the state will ultimately cease to be, this side of eternity it is part of the stable reality of human existence that Christians, no less than any other people, must calculate into their lives.

Those caveats in place, it's worth first noting that Scripture attests to a surprising number of descriptions of the state and a wide number of ways in which God works—including God's grace being mediated through other institutions, not least of which is the state. Isaiah 45 describes God using a Persian king named Cyrus to free the Jewish people from their exile in Babylon; indeed, it goes as far as describing Cyrus—who is, even by scriptural accounts, not especially interested in the well-being of the

Jews—as God's anointed one. And in his letter to the church in Rome, Paul writes that every person should "be subject to the governing authorities; for there is no authority except from God, and those authorities that exist have been instituted by God" (Rom 13:1).

Those texts hardly settle the question of the church's relationship to the state. There are many other scriptural texts that take vastly different positions on the nature of the state and the church's proper relationship to it. The texts simply remind us that we can't rule out the possibility that God's grace works through the state.

All of which returns us to the starting question. Does the church need the state? If so, how? And why? Or, to ask those questions a bit more generally and theologically, what—if any—is the purpose of the state within the economy of God's work in the world?

Three Possible Purposes of the State: Order, Distinctiveness, Training

Christians have given at least three answers to the question of the state's purposes. Thoughtful ones have usually offered up some combination of the three though many Christians seem content to settle on only one. As a result, Christians are almost as likely to disagree about how to think of the state as they are to disagree about how to vote or address a particular social problem. This isn't to say that most Christians don't carry parts of all three of these answers into their political lives. While we may preach conceptual exclusivity, our practices often incorporate portions of all three answers. That's no surprise: in a world that feels as unfinished as ours does, we tend to rely on the tools that we have at hand even if we're not entirely comfortable using the available tools. The processes of disciplined training and leisurely reflection that we rely on when we step back and compare those tools to each other consume more time than we often have when we're feeling around for a tool to use.

Even if we all did have such time for reflection, it wouldn't necessarily be a bad thing if we continued to disagree. Christians have been disagreeing with each other at least since Peter and Paul and there is no reason to think they will stop this side of eternity—especially when the topic under debate is as freighted with emotions and implications as this one is. All three answers, though, have withstood the tests of time and are worth attention.

The first answer is that the state's purpose is to provide order. While this answer transcends any particular denominational perspective, it's especially pronounced in the Roman Catholic tradition as well as parts of the Lutheran and Reformed streams of the Christian faith, all of which have historically emphasized the separate responsibilities that the church and the state have for social welfare. Depending on the personalities and events shaping this answer, providing order can mean maintaining peace via the state's control of the military and the police or maintaining stability via the state's control of the means by which one government succeeds another. Providing order can mean that the state takes on the responsibilities of regulating trade, maintaining oversight of public services, and ensuring safe working conditions or it can mean that the state legislates matters like birth rates and what constitutes a marriage or a family. While the particularities about what providing order means vary from state to state and from age to age—and while many a battle has been fought over where the state's obligation to provide order stops and an individual citizen's freedom begins—the assumption that order is a good thing abides.

Those who affirm this first answer might take as a guiding text the opening lines of 1 Timothy 2: "First of all, then, I urge that supplications, prayers, intercessions, and thanksgiving be made for everyone, for kings and all who are in high positions, so that we may lead a quiet and peaceable life in all godliness and dignity." Among all the people that Christians are called to pray for in this text, only those who are in charge of the state are named. That is especially remarkable given that at the time of its writing, the "kings and all who are in high positions" did not look favorably upon this new religious sect of people calling themselves followers of Christ. Indeed, persecutions of the church, though not constant, were always a threat. And yet even in such a world, the writer of 1 Timothy reminds Christians that their potential persecutors were also the ones who helped to create the conditions that would allow for "a quiet and peaceable life."

All this makes it sound like order is good because it makes life easier for the church. That may be so, but it's hard to read the New Testament and conclude that an easy life is the goal of the church. The church's claims about the goodness of order go back farther than that. They go all the way back to the beginning of the story when God's first acts are described as creating order out of chaos and adding complexity to that order on the way toward making a world that all creatures could live in. And the church's claims about the goodness of order go forward farther than that. They go all the way forward to the end of the story when God's consummating acts are described as recovering order from the forces of chaos and bringing complexity into the harmony of a new heaven and new earth. Making and maintaining order is one of the most significant things God does. Created by an ordering God, we are shaped toward order and inclined toward its benefits. Created in the image of God, we build our lives and our societies in ways to promote order and manage complexity through it. Those who emphasize the state's purpose of providing order are actually describing the state as one of the tools God uses to restrain chaos, maintain complexity, and promote the welfare of creation.

Emphasizing the value of order has important benefits for Christians thinking about how to live in a politically charged world. It reminds us that we cannot be concerned about the spiritual, mental, or physical lives of those around us—the neighbors we have been commanded to love—without also being concerned about the social settings in which they live. After all, while the presence of order won't make people love each other, its absence can make loving each other much harder. That's one of the reasons why many of the greatest reformers of the church and of society—people as varied as Francis of Assisi, Teresa of Avila, John Calvin, Martin Luther King Jr., and Dorothy Day—were so concerned not only with loving their neighbors but with shaping the societies in which those neighbors lived.

This is not to say that order is an unmitigated good. Too much focus on order can lead to a preoccupation with keeping things the way they are—which is hardly a coherent position for anyone who meaningfully prays, "Thy Kingdom come"—and a temptation toward tyranny. It is possible, after all, to have a very orderly but very unjust social system (apartheid South Africa and the segregated south in the U.S. were certainly orderly societies). Moreover, the church has often emphasized order either when it was in a position of political power and so didn't feel the desire to change things or when it felt so powerless that it didn't believe that things could change. Those dangers, though, simply highlight the fact that order isn't the highest good we should seek.

The second answer Christians have given to the question, "What is the purpose of the state?" differs remarkably from the first. It is that the state's purpose is to be an institution against which the church can contrast itself. For some Christians (think, for example, of Old Order Amish), the degree of contrast is extensive. The continued existence of the state is a constant reminder that the Kingdom of God has not yet arrived in all its fullness even as the church's continued faithfulness in both thought and action point to a place in time where the ethics of that Kingdom, inaugurated at Christ's incarnation, are being lived out. For other Christians (think, for example, of some evangelical organizations), the degree of contrast is muted. The state is not only the earthly kingdom from which Christians are drawn but the site of the church's mission to an "unsaved" people. In either case, Christians live as "resident aliens" in the state: we cannot be full members of the state if our allegiance is to a ruler who transcends state boundaries and calls us to transcend national identities.

These Christians might take as their guiding text sections of 1 Peter 2: "But you are a chosen race, a royal priesthood, a holy nation, God's own people, in order that you may proclaim the mighty acts of him who called you out of darkness into his marvelous light . . . For the Lord's sake accept the authority of every human institution, whether of the emperor as supreme or of governors as sent by him to punish those who do wrong and praise those who do right. For it is God's will that by doing right you should silence the ignorance of the foolish." Again, Christians are called to accept the authority of human institutions. But in this case, they do so as a way of revealing their own position *vis a vis* the state: chosen and set apart in order to proclaim the power of God. Indeed, there is not only an explicit condemnation of the foolishness of those who do wrong toward the state but a tacit condemnation of the foolishness of those who do right toward the state because they understand themselves principally as members of the state rather than the Kingdom of God.

All this makes it sound like the church defines itself by what it is not. Yet the emphasis on contrast isn't principally about what the church is against but what it is ultimately for: to be the institution through which the rest of the world sees a glimpse of the Kingdom of God and, in getting such a glimpse, discovers its own destiny. The church is distinctive now—it stands in contrast to the state now—so that it can ultimately lose its distinctiveness as the world, including the state, is transformed into the Kingdom of God. That is why it is so important for the church to live according to a distinct moral vision: its primary job on earth is to be a witness to and model of the world to come. And that's why it ought not take up the various jobs and postures that mark the present world: those jobs and postures are passing away, interim approaches to the problems of the world at best and antithetical to the way life ought to be lived at worst. Where the state uses the coercive powers of violence, the church imagines a world without violence. Where the state seeks to balance competing interests, the church envisions a world in which interests are shared. Where the state thinks of its own preservation, the church embodies a world in which those who would save their lives must lose them. Where power politics and economic might are the coins of the realm, the church says we live by faith, hope and love.

There are important political implications for the Christian belief that the state is a contrast-institution. The emphasis on the distinctiveness of the church ought to remind Christians of the dangers of confusing the goals of the state with those of the church or of attempting to use the tools of the state to achieve their own goals. Indeed, this emphasis on distinctiveness becomes one of the primary arguments in favor of maintaining the separation of church and state: they need to be separated lest the church be seduced into taking up the roles of the state and lose sight of its primary purpose. Moreover, this emphasis on distinctiveness becomes a basis for thinking about how the church does mission. It bears public witness to its own faith and life in the hope that those who see and benefit from that mission will catch a glimpse of the Kingdom into which they are invited. Thus even as the emphasis on distinctiveness shapes an argument in favor of the separation of church and state, it gives reasons for Christians not to separate the public from the private expressions of their faith. We cannot behave differently in different places because we are bearing witness to a single Kingdom; we cannot make faith a private matter because the church only fulfills its purpose when it is behaving in a way that the whole world—including the state—can see. And along the way, by maintaining the public integrity of its witness, the church gains the moral standing to function as a kind of social conscience, reminding the state of what it is not yet and calling the state to learn to behave in ways that will ultimately become its own.

Of course there are problems with this notion of the state as a contrast-institution. Those who affirm this vision of the state undervalue both the biblically affirmed possibility that God can work through the state and also the degree to which the church still exists in this world and is composed of people who sin. The church may be a foretaste of the Kingdom of God but, even so, it isn't a pure taste of that Kingdom. As a result, those who take this approach often magnify the failings of the state while having trouble seeing or addressing their own failings or recognizing their own limitations. They end up with a moral vision that is both cramped and distorted.

Moreover, even though they do not intend to define the church by what it isn't, some who espouse this position sometimes do just that. Whether out of ideological confusion or because it's easier to take methodological shortcuts when thinking about how to behave, they allow their opposition to various practices of the state (e. g., coercion, the use of violence, the promotion of individual rights) to overly shape their own practices. They either withdraw from society or they let protest and resistance become the heart of their engagement with the state and the basis for their social practices. They end up with only a few fairly inflexible approaches to their engagement with the world. And in worst cases, a combination of the first two problems blends to form a toxic mix of cruelty and hypocrisy that not only undermines the credibility of the church's witness but treats many neighbors as deserving of contempt rather than love.

The third answer that Christians have given to the question, "What is the purpose of the state?" is that the state has been given to us by God to train us in becoming Christ's disciples. This answer has been emphasized by diverse groups of Christians throughout time including the Puritans, some contemporary Anglicans, and some Calvinists. For all their differences, though, these groups tend to trace significant aspects of their theological vision to St. Augustine and his great work of political theology, *The City of God*. In that book, Augustine laid out a vision of two "cities" or realms that compete for the hearts of believers: the City of God and the City of Man. A Christian's obligation is to learn to live toward the City of God. The trick, though, is that the two cities cannot be separated according to convenient dichotomies like spiritual vs. political or church vs. state. There is a spirit—albeit a foul one—to the City of Man and a kind of holy politics to the City of God. And one can find evidence of both cities in the church as well as the state.

Augustine argued that though it is immediately easier to live according to the "rules" of the City of Man, Christians' allegiance can ultimately only be to the City of God. Living out that allegiance, though, means learning to see how God is acting in the world and responding appropriately to those actions—which is no small task since our blurred vision regularly causes us to mistake one realm for the other and our desires for our own ease and advancement actively thwart our own efforts to see God at work.

Later theologians like Thomas Aquinas and Karl Barth would pick up on Augustine's vision of the two cities and argue that both the church and the state have a kind of twinned character, partly shaped by and toward good and partly misshaped by sin and evil. Until it is fully transformed by God, the church is an analogue or a reflection of what it will become: the full communion of all the saints with God. Likewise, the state is an analogue or a reflection of what it will become once it is fully transformed: the Kingdom of God. When we think that the current church should only behave as if it were already fully transformed by God, we think too much of it—and then are inevitably disappointed when it fails to act according to our visions of its perfection. Likewise, when we think that current forms of the state are as good as it will get, or when we treat it as nothing more than a stop-gap measure until the time when the state will finally go away, we demand too little of it—and then are strangely disillusioned by it when it only lives up to our too-small visions of its purposes. And just as disappointment leads us to distance ourselves from the church, disillusionment leads us to distance ourselves from the politics of the state. In a kind of double irony, we thereby distance ourselves from the community whose job it is to teach us to see God at work and from the world in which we might look for God at work.

This isn't to say that we should blindly turn back towards either the church or the state. Christians who give this third answer to the purpose of the state harbor no illusions about the sanctity or beneficence of the state. Nor do they harbor illusions about the goodness or purity of the church or themselves. They don't believe that either the church or the state will usher in the Kingdom of God; instead, trusting that God is doing this, they are properly suspicious of all such claims. They don't believe that God works one way in the church and another in the state; instead, they trust God to act in ways that are consistent with how God has always acted: creating, governing, judging, redeeming, and transforming. And they don't believe that God has created the church and the state to focus on different matters; instead, they link spiritual and political matters together in their lives because they witness God doing the same.

Such Christians argue that if God is acting at all, He must be acting in all parts of the world—including the state. They often emphasize Paul's words from the beginning of Romans 13: "Let every person be subject to the governing authorities; for there is no authority except from God, and those authorities that exist have been instituted by God. Therefore whoever resists authority resists what God has appointed, for those who resist will incur judgment . . ." Lest these verses be used as an occasion either for political withdrawal or oppression, though, they are quick to point out that these verses follow from those at the beginning of Chapter 12: "I appeal to you therefore, brothers and sisters, by the mercies of God, to present your bodies as a living sacrifice, holy and acceptable to God, which is your spiritual worship. Do not be conformed to this world, but be transformed by the renewing of your minds, so that you may discern what is the will of God—what is good and acceptable and perfect . . ." It isn't that obedience to authorities should be blind; it's that the transformation of our minds opens our eyes to the way God is working through human authorities.

The task of seeing God work through human authorities is difficult almost to the point of impossibility. Until we are perfected by God we will do it imperfectly. Until the state is perfected by God, we will also see much that is antithetical to God's will. Between now and then, though, we practice at seeing God at work in the state much in the way we practice on a musical instrument or at a sport: perfection is out of our reach but improvement is not. This is both training in a particular way of life and being trained by God in that way and it is what the church has long meant in its doctrine of sanctification. Our participation in the state is both an opportunity for and an inevitable context in which we learn discipleship.

The political implications of the third answer to the question of how to understand the purpose of the state are profound. Those who give this answer treat political engagement not as a choice—as a possible but unseemly addition to their lives to be taken up at the cost of their spiritual maturation—but as the way to pursue that maturation. That is, they participate in politics because it is how they express discipleship. They train themselves to see God at work in the state not so that they can manipulate such wisdom to their own advantage but so that they are more likely to see God at work in the church and in the rest of the world. They train themselves to recognize their own dependence on authorities larger than themselves, not to absolve themselves of responsibility for their actions but so that they are better able to submit themselves to the authority of God. And they train their discontentment with the way things are not to give themselves new opportunities to complain but to remind themselves that their hope must be based in something larger than the seductions of the next political platform or the promises of the next political candidate. They believe that political engagement is more than something that some Christians do; it is what it means to live as a Christian in the first place.

Are their problems with this answer? Certainly—not least of which is the potential for delusion. No matter how earnestly we may try to see God at work, we're just as likely to see only the parts of God's work that conform to our own opinions of how God would act. And when we compensate for that concern—whether by engaging with people who are different from ourselves in order to keep our vision fresh or by withdrawing from the world for a time of self-examination—we're likely to run up against our limits at either putting up with our neighbors or understanding ourselves. But the potential for delusion is only the most significant problem. The more common problem is disappointment borne of our frustration with the speed at which God works. Too much of the time too little seems to be getting better. Impatiently, we force the issues by trying either to make God show Her hand or by trying to take up God's work in our hands. Seeing—and feeling—suffering now, we want that suffering ended now. And the political processes we see around us are either too slow to do that work or are taking a hand in creating that suffering. Reflective discernment and longsuffering patience are not, after all, easy virtues to carry into political engagement. The third problem with this answer is its very difficulty in living out, which not only makes it all-too-easy to turn to either of the first two answers to the question, "What is the purpose of the state?" but also opens one up to the problems that come with those answers.

I imagine it is fairly obvious that I prefer the third answer to the first two. Indeed, in my more argumentative moments (of which there are many—I wrote editorials, after all!) I would go so far as to say the first two answers are but partial expressions of the third. Attention to order gets the importance of the state without understanding the need for the state, itself, to be transformed. Attention to distinctiveness gets the need for change without understanding God's ordained purpose for the state. For Christians, though—who understand themselves as living between the time God created the world and the time God completes the transformation of the world that was begun in the crucifixion and resurrection—living between "the already" and "the not yet" is simply what we do.

That said, there is wisdom in all three answers. Indeed, in my series "Reasons to Stay,"* I tried to pick a particularly acute political problem that the U.S. was facing (when and whether to withdraw troops from Iraq) and address it with an eye to each answer. Thus, the first column advanced an argument about the place of order after the disruptions of 9/11, the second column highlighted my suspicions about the vision and motives of the Bush administration, and the third column at least hinted at ways that we might see some long-term good coming with staying, though such good is likely to be limited and not especially satisfying. I leave it to the reader to answer the question of whether I was successful in either applying the three answers I've summarized above or offering a compelling set of reasons to stay in Iraq. Hopefully, I at least achieved a moment of surprise—a politically liberal argument about staying in Iraq!—that disrupted the settled/stillborn categories of the debate. Such a moment of surprise is, sometimes, enough. Indeed, sometimes it is a sign of hope—which is the virtue to which I now turn.

Hopeful Politics

Political language—and particularly recent political language in the U.S.—is filled with snippets about hope: sound bytes of promises for better days, bigger bank accounts, and brighter futures. Yet conventional wisdom treats contemporary politics as largely a hopeless endeavor. How can this be? Are the purveyors of political rhetoric that out of touch with conventional wisdom? Are they trying to patch over the despairs of the day with high-flung rhetoric or overreaching promises? Have they discovered that such language plays well in our hearts regardless of whether it resonates in our minds? Or, perhaps, are the cures they peddle and assurances they offer not so much expressions of hope but imitations of it?

From a Christian perspective, most of what passes for hope in such rhetoric is, in fact, its opposite: a kind of optimism on steroids, puffed up with its own assurances about the power of the right person, the right group, or the right agenda to change the world. Such language may thrill or inspire us (to be part of the right group, to get involved in such a change, to think as highly about the future as the speechmakers do), but such thrills are short lived and such inspirations soon expire. Neither our awareness of what has happened in the past nor our attention to the magnitude of what is going on around us right now lend credence to such embellishments. Since we live in time, part of us always knows that we can neither separate our future from our past nor our anticipated actions from the ways we actually behave right now. It's not that the past is a horror nor that the present isn't promising nor even that the future can't be better; it's just that neither past nor present give evidence to the kinds of perfection, power, and possibility promised by such fairy-taled optimism. It is ironic that such rhetoric, so often structured around specific promises for concrete expressions of change, is, itself, so unmoored from the lived experiences of those who hear it as they move about in the world: this kind of muscular optimism turns out to be quite literally otherworldly. And our awareness of the false comforts of hypertrophied cheeriness only throws us back into the conditions it was meant to pull us out of: disillusionment, dissatisfaction, delusion, and, ultimately, despair.

Christian hope, on the other hand, begins with attention to past and present. It sees in the past a world that is both deeply flawed and profoundly good—a place God has created and worked in even though that work deeply involved both blessing and sacrifice (indeed, in light of the incarnation, death, and resurrection of Jesus Christ, that work can only be understood as blessing and sacrifice). It sees in the present a world that aches but in which God continues to act. And in light of what it sees, it tries to imagine a future that can account for all of this—for both goodness and the awareness that this isn't yet good enough; for both limitation and the sense that these limitations, too, have a limit; for both an appreciation for all that God has done and a conviction that God is not yet done. So often accused of being otherworldly, Christian hope turns out to be far more grounded in time and anchored in a profound understanding of this world as it actually is than the various imitations of hope that pass for good news in most political discourse. Hope, then, isn't so much an action we initiate as a vision that motivates and gives direction to our actions.

Among the clearer ways to distinguish Christian hope from its poor imitations is the way it structures our understanding of what counts as good news. The imitations promise us that with enough effort and ingenuity, all our problems will be solved; Christian hope reminds us that our problems are beyond our capacity to repair but not beyond God's ability to redeem. That is, Christian hope is not utopian and so it helps us avoid the overly simple falsities of "If we do x then y will happen." The imitations promise us that we can sit back and let others take care of our problems; Christian hope reminds us that we are participants in the problems and actors in the world and so our actions are both problematic and also matter. That is, Christian hope is not passive and so helps us resist the tempting miseries of "There's nothing we can do." Hope reminds us that history is littered with futile utopian projects, disastrous attempts at quietism, and, above all, the bodies of those who suffered from the failures to either end history or step outside of it.

This isn't to say that hope is an easy thing to do. The tension between seeing the world as it is (and ourselves as we are) and feeling what the world ought to be (and how we will be in that world) is almost unbearable. And while it may be of some comfort to realize that this tension is mirrored in the central conflict of political life (i.e., the conflict between the public good that is the goal of politics and the corrupted procedures that are the means we have to work for that goal), such comfort is often cold. Undoubtedly one of the reasons that we accept the popular political rhetorics of hope is that it relieves us of that tension by either describing the world (and us) as we are not or by offering what the world ought to be as an immediately impending historical reality.

It is the very difficulty of hope that makes Christian community necessary. We need the support of others when hope fades, the encouragement of others when we'd rather ignore hope, the examples of others when we don't know how to hope. And while life in Christian community is as likely to be caught up in the imitations of hope as any other community, its common text and historical memory provide us with regular reminders of hope's power (from God's promises to Abraham and Israel and the birth of the church out of a scattered and frightened group of disciples to the end of slavery and the power of the Civil Rights movement to overturn segregation)—not to mention the community's repeated and insistent calls that we not confuse poor imitations of hope with the real thing.

Given the examples of the previous paragraph (not to mention the establishment of human rights, the destruction of various twentieth-century fascisms, the collapse of the Berlin Wall, the end of Apartheid in South Africa . . .), it is apparent that hope can motivate political activity. But how does a Christian understanding of hope shape our political activities?

First, it encourages us to be patient. Many of us in Western cultures have become willing victims to a noxious attitude that combines the awareness of the magnitude and scope of problems around the world with a culture of immediate gratification. Hearing daily of tragedies and horrors around the world, we want them fixed immediately. While this combination may repeatedly stimulate our individual and collective passions to do something, it can't nourish those passions; it turns us into political manic-depressives, cycling wildly between establishing great plans to transform the world and despairing that the world will never change. After a while, a kind of faux-cynicism sets in, not because we've decided to give up but because we need something to inoculate ourselves against the pain of swinging between illusory hope and transient despondency.

Patience insists that we take the time to reflect on both the problems and our own desires (which is one of the reasons it isn't an easy thing to learn: the things we discover about ourselves and our relation to the world aren't always pleasant). In so doing, patience tempers our political mood-swings by training us not to orient the world's problems around our own needs and desires. It reminds us that we're too small to contain the solutions to those problems within ourselves and too implicated in those problems to think that we are part of the solution but not part of the problem. And in re-orienting us to ourselves and the problems, it creates the space we need to envision the long slow processes in which God is working in the world and imagine how to respond to those processes.

Several years ago I was teaching a course in South Africa on the role of religion in the Truth and Reconciliation Commission there. While there, the class took a field trip to Robben Island, the prison off the coast of Cape Town where Nelson Mandela and other political prisoners had been held. By coincidence, several of us happened to be on a bus with a man named Andrew Mlangeni. As a young man, Mlangeni was active in the African National Congress's attempt to overturn the Apartheid regime and, with Mandela, was one of the "Rivonia Ten," the group of defendants sentenced to life imprisonment on Robben Island for crimes against the state. Now a Member of Parliament, he was visiting his former prison that day, showing members of his wife's family where he'd spent a quarter century of his life. I asked him what had sustained him during all that time. He told me, "We always knew that when the rest of the world heard about what was going on in South Africa, they would apply enough pressure on the government to help us overturn the regime. We just had to keep making our case known and wait. We thought it would take about five years." He laughed. "We were right! International pressure did help us end apartheid! Of course, our time table was off by about two decades!"

Mlangeni, Mandela, and the others who spent decades on Robben Island imagined an end to apartheid that was bigger than anything their own actions could achieve. On Robben Island, where they couldn't change the world, they could start to learn how to live in a post-apartheid South Africa. They shared their stories with each other and smuggled bits of those stories out to the half-observant world. They worked at getting the various imprisoned members of rival political factions to live together. They slowly built relationships with many of the guards. They did the small things and trusted that greater powers could do the bigger things. And after apartheid ended, the former prisoners and former guards worked together to turn Robben Island into a national historic site so that people from all over the world could come to see a symbol not only of the historic costs of racial separation but of the current possibilities of racial cooperation as well.

Along the way, patience reminds us (sometimes repeatedly) that we shouldn't see being small as a tragic sign of our limitations but as a relief from the idea that it's our job to make history come out right. Relieved of burdens that a realistic appraisal of history suggests cannot be ours, we are freed to take on the responsibilities that are ours. Indeed, this is a second part of how a Christian vision of hope shapes a political vision: it unburdens us from the overweening sense of responsibility that comes with a hypertrophied sense of self. Christian hope is shaped not by the desire to enlarge our own powers but by the search for a power that is large enough to overcome our distended desires in the process (and as an aspect) of transforming the world.

And this, in turn, orients and empowers the Christian's ability to speak prophetically about the world around it. Prophetic speaking is properly neither a project of forecasting the future (though it carries within itself the conviction that there is a future worth attending to) nor condemning present injustice (though it treats present injustice as evidence about what stands between the present and that future). Instead, the prophet's deepest claim is that the world neither has been nor will be bereft of a righteous God, with all the threat and promise that such divine presence entails.

Christian prophetic speakers, then, gain their voice when they stand between present injustice and future glory: bound to the present by their recognition of their small and conflicted but nonetheless meaningful place in the world, they can grieve its injustice without damning it. Shaped by their vision of the future and clearer of their place in it, they can work for justice without being overwhelmed by their failures. Seeking to discern and then describe the will of God, they therein bring the deeply theological language of judgment and reconciliation to public consciousness. In all this, hope and prophetic voice are inextricably bound: prophetic voice without hope is unrestrained doomsaying and hope without prophetic voice is willful naivety.

One regular by-product of this patient, relieved, prophetic conception of hope is surprise. Whether because of how easily we settle into the most convenient vision of the world around us or how often we discover that our thoughts are not God's thoughts and our ways are not God's ways, hope perpetually catches us off-guard. (Could there be two more surprising and yet hopeful moments in all of human history than the incarnation and the resurrection??) So part of living in hope means living a little off balance and part of expressing a hopeful politics is trying to describe the world in ways that disrupt listeners' settled visions of things. It's not that all surprises are hopeful but that hope is perpetually surprising.

In the introductory chapter, I suggested that I wrote editorials the way Emily Dickinson wrote poetry: on a slant. That was my way of trying to exemplify hopeful politics. I tried to view the world on a slant—to catch it in my peripheral vision rather than look straight at it—because I believe that the hopeless views of the world that pass either for realism or optimism are not only inaccurate but inhibit accuracy. God's actions in the world may be the most significant and intentional events in it, but they aren't easy to see and, shorn of a kind of faithfulness like that described in chapter 2, they are too easily ignored or denied. Saying something surprising or writing on a surprising topic was my way of trying to help others see differently. I think my best editorials were also my most surprising ones.

Unfortunately, that usually meant letting surprise substitute for hope. Occasionally, though, it meant actually saying something hopeful. So I sometimes picked overlooked stories that I thought needed more attention—like an editorial on "A Common Word Between You and Us,"* the remarkable statement about the relationship between Islam and Christianity that was generated by a group of leading Islamic clerics and scholars and garnered far less attention than I thought it deserved. At other times, I picked overinflated and stale debates and tried to re-describe them—like the twin editorials on health care, "Debating Health Care"* and "Still Debating Health Care"*—not in order to offer a solution to their problems but to push against the stolid and unhelpful approaches that I believed characterized them. (I was reminded of another lesson about speaking in the public sphere after the first of the health care articles came out. It drew a vitriolic response from one letter-writer who claimed my arguments were injurious to doctors and vaguely communist. I can only assume he read all this into the final sentence of that article—in which I suggested that there were benefits to the health care plan rejected by Congress in 1994—since my actual arguments had no immediate implications for doctors and nothing to do with communism. Given enough passion and bias, people can read what they want to read into almost anything. I suppose this is further reason to be grateful for a Christian vision of hope in which everything doesn't rest on the human ability to read in an unbiased way or write in a universally compelling way.)

This side of eternity, real problems aren't likely to admit to permanent solutions that will satisfy everyone—and even if they were, I couldn't imagine an 800-word essay that could describe such a solution. But, again, there is a kind of relief in realizing that: freed from the obligation to solve it all and put a bow on it, I could write editorials that were obviously incomplete. Sometimes saying something surprising is enough—or at least it's a start toward thinking hopefully.

Spectatorial Politics (Redux)

Return to my comments about spectatorial politics at the beginning of this chapter. I suggested there that we engage in politics in a way analogous to our engagement with a favorite sports team. And I suggested that spectatorial politics betrays our confusion about how to think about politics but that it might not be all bad (and it might be the shadowy product of some very fortunate things that have happened to many of us). Indeed, I imagine that until enough people face enough hardship in trying to supply their basic material needs, the specter of spectators is likely to continue: it's hard for most of us to work up enough energy to get involved in political arguments about differences of opinion regarding cultural symbols, status, and recognition.

Some political systems don't allow citizens to get involved in government—but that's not the case in most Western countries. Some political systems don't have the resources to ensure that most of their citizens' basic needs are met—but that's not the case in many Western countries. Many of the most vociferous fights in economically stable democratic countries (e.g., fights over abortion, gay rights, and race relations) exist, in part, because we have the stability and leisure to have them. It's no wonder that politics is spectatorial.

Yet beyond the fact that we're political spectators because we can be, I wonder if one of the reasons that we've turned into watchers is that we've drained politics of surprise. Candidates for office are carefully manicured and given a mandate to stay on message if they want to win. The news media tends toward sound-byte analysis and a focus on the races themselves, turning politicians into ciphers that must represent the predetermined positions of their parties. The professionalized punditry have largely lost interest in the independence of their own ideas and become apologists for branded thoughts, mouthing the very talking points that they ought to be breaking down. The only surprises worth attention are scandalous. We vote for incumbents not only because we value experience and the expertise it brings but because we are soothed by the status quo. And nobody is willing to say, "I don't know what will happen next." Our spectatorial approach has made us preoccupied with elections and our antipathy for surprise has given us candidates for office and elected officials who are, quite literally, hopeless.

As long as we're preoccupied with treating engagement in democratic politics as the project of getting the right leaders, we're likely to continue to face such hopelessness. But, as I tried to argue in a series of editorials on the dangers of thinking too much about the quality of leadership among political candidates (the last of which is "Dangled Mirages"*), constitutional democracies aren't principally about leadership. They're about public engagement—about reading newspapers and participating in civic groups (including churches) and writing letters to the editor and trying to get speed bumps installed on neighborhood streets and campaigning for cleaner water and supporting our local police and fire departments and volunteering our time to mentor children in after-school programs and arguing with our colleagues about politics over lunch and finding other constructive ways to let our voices be heard as well as going to the polls on election day. And once we get it through our heads that constitutional democracies are not about leadership, they become far more interesting things.

Part of what makes them interesting is that they're shaped to both respond to the new and surprising (hence regular elections and an always-revisable constitution) and to stabilize the repercussions of surprise in order to avoid their more damaging consequences (hence the emphasis on fair procedures and rule of law). Among available political systems, at least, constitutional democracies are amenable to novelty, surprise, and saying, "I don't know" in a way that others aren't. And while their citizens may feel "Stuck in the Muddle"* of processes that are never as smooth as they'd like nor as certain as they'd wish, they can nonetheless move forward not only in spite of the muddle but because of it.

Christian hope, I should be quick to point out, isn't in democracy; it is in salvation through the mighty acts of God. But Christians in a constitutional democracy can let hope shape their politics precisely because such a political system creates a wide and generous space in which citizens can imagine something new or see something not everyone notices. And they can be participants rather than spectators because they can see that they're responders rather than initiators of action.

Perhaps I'm being too harsh on spectatorial politics. Perhaps being a political spectator isn't an entirely bad thing. After all, spectators are more than observers. They not only pay attention; they care. And because they care, they participate, albeit in ways that are unlikely to induce any interesting or beneficial changes in the public sphere. It's a kind of passionate running in place, too worked up to quit and too confused or satisfied to move forward. Ultimately, it's exhausting—like reading journal after journal and skimming newspaper after newspaper and watching news report after news report, all to find the right insight into the right topic on which to write a maximum of 800 words.

Perhaps, moreover, the disconnect between caring about political matters and working to change them is a sign worth interpreting. It strikes me that although it isn't the whole of the matter, spectatorial politics is marked by participation without anticipation. It neither sees evidence that something profoundly good is going on nor imagines a world in which things could be genuinely better.

All of that, though, makes a Christian vision of hopeful politics—and a hopeful Christian engagement with politics—so much more valuable. As a faith, Christianity doesn't believe that it contains cures to the world's ills (or even the neighborhood's ills): it believes God does that. As a church, Christians don't believe their perspective on political matters is the only one or even that their perspective must dominate: God, not the church, ultimately practices dominion in the world. However, they can infuse hope into politics. Along the way, they may help shape spectators more fully into citizens and citizens more openly into inquirers about what is really going on in the world. It may not be the church's job to create better citizens for the states of the world but it is its job to be public, to be confessional, to believe that God is transforming the world, and to respond to that transforming work by being trained in hope.

Identity Politics

(Appeared June 17, 2007)

In what some would construe as an attempt to court liberal favor, President Bush has taken yet another swipe at Christians by nominating James Holsinger as surgeon general.

That sentence sounded odd, didn't it? Perhaps I should explain. Dr. Holsinger, a cardiologist from Kentucky, is the Duke University-trained, former secretary of health for the state of Kentucky and chancellor of the University of Kentucky's medical center. He's taught at multiple medical schools and was in the Army Reserve for over three decades before retiring as a major general. He's a devout Methodist and has a Master's degree from Asbury Theological Seminary. And in 1991 he argued that gay sex is unnatural and unhealthy. He's also voted to expel a lesbian pastor from the United Methodist Church.

It's those last bits that have drawn the ire of gay rights groups, who argue that his positions on gay sex and the ordination of gays and lesbians are ideologically flawed and medically inaccurate. Medical understandings of homosexuality have changed since 1991—though not so much that much of what science says today was unheard of then—so maybe we can ignore the '91 paper (depending on what he has to say about things today; unfortunately, he's not saying anything right now). And ecclesial politics in mainline denominations surrounding gay and lesbian ordination are a maelstrom of contending and painfully loud voices—so maybe we can let that one slide. But before giving him the pass, we ought to attend to how he's being defended against his critics.

The argument made by those defending his nomination runs along these lines: regardless of what Holsinger may personally think about gays and lesbians, he won't let those personal positions get in the way of his work. As surgeon general, he'll be able to separate his own beliefs from the work that comes with the office. So don't worry, gay rights advocates: this guy won't let his religious convictions get in the way of doing the job.

That's what worries me.

His defenders would treat his religious convictions as epiphenomena; a set of beliefs that he can hold in some contexts but that he can ignore (or cast off) in others. Maybe the significance of his faith is a part of what makes him an interesting appointment (how many other surgeon generals have a seminary degree, after all?) but he can cordon it off through some type of psychological apartheid when needed. One wonders: would his defenders say the same thing about his medical convictions? That at the end of the day when he takes the stethoscope off, he won't think like a doctor anymore?

There used to be a term for the philosophical position that one could segregate one's personal and public convictions so that the two didn't conflict when faced with political matters. The term was "liberal"—a term that has long since been transformed to mean something else (or, more properly, lots of other things, depending on who says it). Holsinger's supporters are advancing a liberal defense—albeit one that, ironically, social conservatives won't see in their rush to support a conservative Methodist to the post of surgeon general.

But as both religious and secular political philosophers have long pointed out, the problem with the idea-formerly-known-as-liberalism is that it doesn't accurately describe the complex ways identity works. And it especially doesn't describe the way most genuinely religious people think about their religious convictions; namely, as things that pervade every aspect of their identity and have the potential to shape all their thoughts and actions.

There is no administrative appointment that is more likely to face questions of identity than that of surgeon general for the simple fact that so many of the problems that modern science and medicine face are caught up in those questions. How shall we think about embryos? Or stem cell therapies (which Holsinger supports, by the way)? Or genetic modification? Or abortion? Or when to declare someone dead or whether to think of a medical condition like deafness as a disability or when reconstructive surgery is principally cosmetic or the impact of prescribing behavior-modifying drugs, or . . . or . . . or . . . A perspective that thinks it's adequate to begin a statement with "Though I'm a devout Christian, I can ignore the totalizing demands that faith makes on me in order to do the job" isn't likely to be adequate to deal with those questions.

His opponents are worried that Holsinger won't be able to shelve his faith when acting as Attorney General. We ought to be worried if he thinks he can.

Two Cheers for Partisanship
(Appeared July 1, 2007)

New York City mayor Michael Bloomberg has recently announced his departure from the Republican Party to become an Independent, perhaps in anticipation of a run for the presidency. We might have predicted it: he left the Democratic Party for the Republican one in order to become mayor and it's not like his political inclinations mesh especially well with those of the contemporary Republican Party. Perhaps, unlike the old Tareyton cigarette smokers, he'd rather switch than fight.

More likely, though, he'd rather switch *to* fight. His decision to leave the Republican Party was generated, in part, by an attempt to clear some space for himself as someone who doesn't believe in partisanship. It might work (at least to the degree that any independent candidacy works). Polls show that Americans are frustrated with partisan fighting in Washington—so much so that Congressional approval ratings are actually lower than those of President Bush. Whether this frustration is borne of Congress' seeming failure to get much done (which isn't exactly true, anyway), a "why can't we all just get along?"

idealism, a suspicion of political processes more generally, or something else, I don't know. But I want to give two cheers for partisanship.

The first cheer: partisanship is evidence of political memory. None of us—including our elected leaders—can handle the massive amounts of data associated with all the political issues of the day. Instead, we rely on those around us who have wisdom in particular areas to inform us of the issues. And those around us, in turn, rely on experts who have done such work before them, building upon and modifying the wisdom of the past to fit it to our current context. And this, in a nutshell, is what political parties are: repositories of political memory. Since none of the most important issues we face can be simply and clearly resolved in ways that will satisfy everyone (after all, if they could be resolved like this, they already would have been), we should expect that wisdom on such matters is not uniform and does not speak in a single voice. So there will be more than one party, more than one approach, more than one vision, and more than one memory. Partisanship is the result of contending memories and contending memories, while frustrating, are better than no memory at all.

The second cheer: partisanship is a product of passion. Who would you rather have represent you in office: someone who is just killing time while there or someone who really gives a damn about what's going on and wants to effect change? Where apathy is among the greatest of threats to functioning constitutional democracy, a little passion is certainly a good thing. Think of it this way: partisanship at least gives our elected officials something to do—and keeping them busy keeps them in the public eye where we can keep an eye on them—which, in turn, keeps them at least somewhat out of trouble. Would that more people were partisan! It would at least be a signal that they cared about what happened around them.

So: two cheers for partisanship. But only two. The failings of partisanship—like the failings of most good things—are the dark sides of its virtues. Partisanship may be evidence of political memory, but when it outgrows its purpose, its antagonistic system can induce its own kind of political amnesia in which political parties focus only on maintaining their values rather than ordering them. And in the process, partisanship replaces a passion for addressing political issues with a passion for defeating the other guys. The simplistic attitude of "we're against whatever they're for and we're for whatever they're against" helps nobody. And in contemporary U.S. politics, these dark sides are all too prevalent.

But why should this surprise us? Aren't the current failings of partisanship symptomatically identical to the anti-partisan bias that Bloomberg and others are trading on? Isn't our frustration with partisanship, itself, an expression of a "we're against whatever they're for" attitude? And isn't it indicative of our own historical amnesia—a kind of insistence that we could do it better on our own?

I wish Bloomberg and the people of New York City luck. I really do. But more than luck, they—and all of us, really—need wisdom and passion. And for those resources, we better be willing to accept a bit of partisanship in our politics. Now if we can just use wisdom and passion to help us do a better job at being partisan.

A Reason to Stay, Part One: Casus belli

(Appeared February 18, 2007)

The situation in Iraq has turned Joe Strummer into a prophet. As front man for The Clash, he sang, "If I go there will be trouble. An' if I stay it will be double." Since most Democrats and a growing number of Republicans think that trouble beats double, leaving seems likely. Indeed, given the direction the war is heading (beyond civil war into anarchy), the repeated failures of the war plan, the growing number of U.S. casualties and falling popular support for staying, withdrawal increasingly seems not only viable but imminent.

The fact that only President Bush's most ardent supporters and those furthest to the right are saying we ought to stay isn't helping matters: as the political pendulum swings back toward the center, their arguments seem less and less reasonable or connected to the facts on the ground. This is unfortunate, since there are important reasons to stay—though the only people likely to embrace these reasons are the very Democrats calling for withdrawal.

To understand why we ought to stay, though, it's necessary to look backwards and see why we're there in the first place. The Bush Administration gave reason after reason for the war:

- Iraq was developing WMD's (anthrax, yellowcake from Niger . . .).
- Iraq was in defiance of United Nations resolutions.
- Saddam Hussein could be connected to *Al Queda* and, thereby to 9/11.
- We would be furthering the cause of freedom and bringing democracy to the region.
- A stable, democratic Iraq would lead to the creation of other stable democracies in the Middle East.
- The Baathist regime was responsible for countless atrocities against Iraqi citizens.
- It would lead to a more stable and open oil market, thereby promoting economic stability worldwide.

Whether advanced individually and collectively, these were *casus belli*. Since the start of the war, most of those reasons have disappeared in puffs of gun smoke or under the harsh light of realism. But there is one other reason that the greatest superpower and most

successful democracy in world history invaded Iraq, and that reason has been systematically ignored and therefore has gone substantially unchallenged: namely, we wanted to.

Polls taken in the lead-up to the war showed between two thirds and three fourths of Americans supporting the decision to invade. Without that type of popular support, it is unlikely that plans for the war—or at least the particular plans for this war—would have gone forward. But why was there such popular support? I'd argue that the reasons didn't lead to such support; they simply made such support tenable. That is, the reasons just gave us rational excuses for doing what we wanted to do anyway. But as social scientists have long pointed out, human beings—especially when thinking as a group—aren't rational animals so much as rationalizing ones.

Americans were looking for something to do with their continued public anger at what happened on September 11, 2001, and their substantial public fear at something like those events—or worse—recurring. Absent either something else about which to be angrier and more fearful or some force that would make expressing that anger, fear, mourning, or desire for revenge prohibitive, popular support, in itself, became a *casus belli*—perhaps the principal one. And as the world's only true superpower, there weren't other forces to make cathartic action on our part prohibitive.

Because this has been a cathartic war. That's why we still haven't come up with any adequate means for protecting our ports, distributing Homeland Security funds to vulnerable populations, dealing with the conditions that produce terrorism, or responding to radical Islam. The war's cathartic origins continue to make most debates about border security and immigration useless and some of them xenophobic. Its cathartic origins play a role in promoting the viscerally-charged partisan politics that have so troubled us. And these same origins explain why public support for a war that was always going to cause death and destruction (as all wars do) and always going to be long (as even Donald Rumsfeld warned us) has evaporated. If you think this war is a mistake—and especially if you thought it was a good idea in 2003—you ought to admit that the war isn't "their fault." It's ours. But I doubt we'll admit that.

We've reviewed, debated, and otherwise manipulated the reasons for war provided by the Bush administration in 2003. We have not, however, dealt with the degree to which public support made the war possible. Nor have we explored the cathartic origins of that public support. And since we don't seem interested in such explorations, the only thing that is going to keep us from a new war the next time we feel so angry, fearful, and vengeful is going to be an awareness that we can't pay the prices that come with it. Said differently, the thing most likely to keep us out of a new war is that we're still dealing with the present one. Leaving the disaster of Iraq, however, will make it more possible for us to enter a new one.

And here's the problem: the new tragedy-demanding-a-response is waiting just around the historical corner. The new reasons to support that response are already being developed. And the new enemy is already being named. It's Iran.

A Reason to Stay, Part 2: On Not Leaving Old Wars for New Ones

(Appeared February 25, 2007)

Last week I suggested three things: That the Iraq war was made possible by popular support for going to war; that this popular support was connected to our need to do something with the fear, anger, and confusion we felt after 9/11; and that as a society we hadn't yet—and were unlikely to—confront the cathartic origins of the war. I also argued that our unchallenged cathartic motives could push us back into war should the need for such catharsis arise again and that the most likely place they would rear their heads had to do with U.S.-Iranian relations.

Since a U.S. decision to leave Iraq would have the effect of freeing up American troops and allowing us to change the focus of our Middle East foreign policy—and since U.S.-Iranian relations are moving in increasingly confrontational directions—anyone (read: "Democrats") interested in preventing a larger war in the Middle East should think again about withdrawing from Iraq.

What makes Iran such a problem? Perhaps surprisingly, it isn't

their president. While he has done a great deal to stir up trouble internationally, Mahmoud Ahmadinejad has neither the political power nor the popular support in Iran to drive Iranian policy. Instead, Iran will be a problem primarily because its national self-interest will, predictably, drive it toward increased involvement in Iraq.

Iran has no interest in living next to an anarchic state. Not only would instability in Iraq have the effect of sending tens of thousands of refugees streaming across its border but, to the extent that Iraqi instability turns on ethnic conflicts, Iran has good reason to be concerned about the expansion of those conflicts into Iran. Though predominantly Shiite, Iran has significant Kurdish and Sunni minorities—as well as numerous other rebellious minority groups—within its borders already. If those groups favor ethnic over national identity (as many already do) Iran will face growing unrest within its borders. Even more problematically, unrest in Iran is already most visible among the startlingly high percentage of young and unemployed men—the very group most likely to turn toward violence directed at either its own government or another government. And it's not as if Iranian-Iraqi relations were good to start out with: the war that raged between those two countries in the 1980s is still a live memory for many Iranians.

And these problems of national self-interest are compounded by Iranian aspirations. Iran wants to be a dominant player in Middle Eastern politics; hence, their interest in developing nuclear weapons and their bellicosity toward what they perceive as Western imperialism. Having weathered both internal reformist challenges and external opprobrium over the past several years, Iran is now feeling stronger and more assertive than it has for years—as its participation in last summer's Israel-Lebanon conflict reveals.

In short, Iran is both properly concerned about domestic stability and proudly feeling its international oats—a combination that makes it dangerously confrontational and inclined toward international action, especially in Iraq and Israel, which are also the two countries most linked to the U.S. Indeed, the surprise isn't that Iran might be supplying weapons to Shiite militia in Iraq; it's that it isn't interfering in Iraq in bigger and more obvious ways.

What makes all this even more complicated and troublesome

is that it is unlikely that the Bush Administration is willing to accept a legacy framed by failure in Iraq and non-responsiveness to Iranian bellicosity—especially since U.S. interests will continue to intersect with the Middle East for the foreseeable future. Moreover, given current U.S.-Iran relations and popular U.S. perceptions of Iran, any aggressively bellicose act by Iran in Iraq, against Israel, or toward the U.S. and its troops is likely to trigger the very type of popular U.S. attitudes that made the current war possible. And given actual Iranian national interests and aggressiveness, this time there won't be any need to manipulate evidence of perceived malfeasance to garner support for war.

As a result, the only thing that is especially likely to keep the U.S. from focusing its political, economic, and military energies on Iran is that such energies are already preoccupied. And right now, they're preoccupied with Iraq.

All of which makes debates and non-binding resolutions about the surge misplaced. The surge is unlikely to achieve stability in Iraq, though it might help a little bit. And at this point, U.S. withdrawal is unlikely to achieve that stability though it might hurt Iraq quite a bit, making it even more likely that Iraq will go from tyranny to anarchy in the space of five years (thereby making it even more likely that Iran will feel compelled to act). The danger is that if the surge fails to live up to its billing of bringing stability to Iraq—which is likely—it may provide an excuse to withdraw: "We've done everything we can and the Iraqis have refused to work together; therefore, we'll stop wasting our energy and soldiers there." But while withdrawal may feel like the right thing to do with respect to Iraq, it may prove to be the exact wrong thing to do with respect to preventing a larger conflict with Iran.

A Reason to Stay, Part 3: The Hard Work of Diplomacy

(Appeared March 5, 2007)

Secretary of State Condoleezza Rice recently told the Iranian government that we would talk with them only if they stopped enriching uranium. She *told* them this. This isn't so much a failed effort at the silent treatment as one of the funkier steps in the dance of diplomacy. But is it a dance interesting enough for the Iranians to join in? The Iranian government has already suggested that it would suspend its enrichment program if Western nations would do so as well. Yeah: that's likely.

So is the U.S. in a standoff with Iran? Are the only things that distinguish this from a scene in a Sergio Leone movie the absence of a good soundtrack and the fact that nobody's actually standing still? Iran is still enriching uranium in the face of growing U.N. sanctions and the U.S. is still fighting wars on either side of Iran even as it sends more ships into the area. Right now it certainly seems Leone-esque. The next scene would be fascinating were some of its implications not so horrifying. And in the face of that potential horror, we need to be asking not about present actions, but about the ones after that: what are likely responses to our actions and how might we respond to those responses?

For the past two weeks, I have been attempting to draw out one increasingly likely answer to that question. As the U.S. and its allies either withdraw or consider withdrawal and as Iran continues to expand its power in the Middle East, we should not only expect that Iran will enter into the power vacuum created by withdrawal but we should expect that those movements are likely to result in hostilities between the two countries. And if hostilities become too pronounced, the same U.S. public that made the war in Iraq possible may end up calling for a new war. Ironically, then, staying in Iraq may be one of the best ways to prevent an escalation toward war with Iran.

This is not to say that staying in Iraq will make things hunky-dory with Iran. Indeed, staying in Iraq will have the likely result of exacerbating tensions with Iran. Whether the U.S. likes it or not, the Iranian presence in Iraq is going to increase both overtly or covertly—especially as British troops withdraw from Shiite-dominant southern Iraq. And since the U.S. has been clear that it does not like the idea of Iranian involvement, that involvement is going to make for some toughgoing. Conflict is probable and things are

likely to get worse before they get better. Jockeying for political position among militias would likely lead to proxy skirmishes. Conflicting U.S. and Iranian goals with regard to Iraqi sovereignty will make resolving those conflicts difficult.

But if conflict is likely either way, it behooves us to think about comparative levels of violence. Proxy skirmishes are better than shock-and-awe, invasion, and counter-attacks that would likely embroil other countries. This will especially be the case as Iran continues to move toward being a nuclear threat. The use of WMD's or preemptive actions to prevent their use would almost certainly catch other countries (Israel, Syria, Saudi Arabia) up in the conflict. Better in for this penny now than in for that pound later. Moreover, Iran's desire to be a player on the international scene may actually have the effect of limiting such skirmishes since if they really want to show their power, they'll have to do better than hiding behind Shiite militia in Iraq the way they hid behind Hezbollah last summer in Lebanon.

It also behooves us to think about how to mitigate violence where possible, and the first lesson of mitigating violence is to establish points of concurrence between parties. A U.S. withdrawal from Iraq will not end U.S. interests in the Middle East. It will, however, shut us off from a matter of concern currently shared with Iran; namely, Iraqi stability. It wouldn't be the first time that the U.S. and Iran worked together even as they resisted improved relations: Iran supported the decision to remove the Taliban from Afghanistan. Moreover, recognizing this gives the U.S. a significant diplomatic card to play. Combine that card with the fact that staying in Iraq puts our armed forces on either side of Iran and U.S. diplomats have both a carrot and a stick.

This still won't make for easy diplomacy. But then, diplomacy never really is easy. It can be much more complicated than resorting to violence and it can produce results that are less-than-satisfying to ideologues who can imagine no way but their own. In the face of spiraling violence and the repeated failures of ideologies though, diplomacy is a pretty good alternative. At this point, talking is both wiser than not doing so and more courageous than saber-rattling.

So set aside dead-ended "I'm not talking to you" rhetoric. And set aside facile debates about nonbinding resolutions on the surge. And set aside naive claims that

Democrats favor withdrawal and Republicans don't. The issue isn't what's going on in Iraq right now; it's what's likely to go on in the future as both Iraq and the countries that surround it respond to U.S. actions there. The topic shouldn't be what withdrawal accomplishes; it should be what withdrawal initiates. And in the face of the calamity that could follow from withdrawal, staying in Iraq—frustrating and tragic as it may be—may be the wiser thing to do.

An Uncommon Word

(Appeared November 4, 2007)

Last month, a group of 138 Muslim scholars, theologians, and clerics from all over the world—including grand muftis from most Islamic countries as well as many other influential clerics and scholars representing all the major branches of Islam—issued an open letter to Christians, which they titled "A Common Word Between You and Us." In the letter, they emphasized the common moral starting points of the world's two most populous religions (namely love of God and love of neighbor), and the importance of those moral starting points not only for inter-religious dialogue but in working toward peace and justice around the world.

Since Islam doesn't have a co-ordinated polity or central office, it's a bit hard to signify the importance of this letter or the weightiness of its signers. This is a group of Islamic heavyweights whose coming to-gether is decidedly uncommon, as is their agreement with the text. The list of recipients, though—Pope Benedict XVI, every Orthodox patriarch, the Archbishop of Canterbury, and heads of most ma-jor mainline denominations both in the U.S. and abroad—and the fact

that most of those recipients have responded—give some sense of its weight. For Christian-Islamic rela-tions this is a big deal and it comes at a time fraught with religious and political implications for those rela-tions, not to mention the degree to which those relations are fraught with political implications.

Did you hear about it?

If you were like most folks I've talked with, probably not. It made the news—briefly—when it came out, though coverage varied from the laudatory to the alarmist (Reuters: "Unprecedented Muslim call for peace with Christians"; Washington Post: "Muslim Leaders Call for Interfaith Peace"; Fox News: "Muslim Leaders Warn Pope 'Survival of World' at Stake"). Since the initial flurry of articles, though, attention has waned on the parts of all except a few academics and those committed to interfaith relations.

So what's the bigger story? That the letter came out? Or that it received so little attention from so many in the West?

It certainly ought to be a big story that the letter came out—in some ways, even bigger than the release of a papal encyclical, if only because the structural clarity of the Roman Catholic Church makes producing encyclicals comparatively easy and because we expect encyclicals to float across our experiential horizons every once in a while. At the same time, since "A Common Word" doesn't go very far in addressing the various causes of unrest between the "Muslim" and "Christian" worlds, the letter may not make for interesting news. Ultimately, the letter's newsworthiness will probably be determined more by its still-unknown implications than by its initial existence.

Perhaps, the comparison to a papal encyclical is instructive in a different way: their release doesn't stir up sustained public interest either. Unless you're a devout Roman Catholic or, again, an academic, your attention to them probably lags as well. Do you remember *Deus Caritas Est* from 2005?

But do our cultural tune-deafness to religion and our concomitant preoccupation with all its hollow imitations (e.g., therapeutic egocentrism, rococo nationalism, and partisan evangelicalism) adequately explain the failure of "A Common Word" to make a noise? I doubt it, because we've become quite interested in Islam in the last six years. Even though few of you heard about "A Common Word," I bet most of you have heard some version of the question, "Why

don't we hear Muslims responding to events like suicide bombings in Iraq and Palestine and opinions expressed by Islamic radicals?"

I hear it regularly in the courses I teach whose topics intersect contemporary world politics. Usually, it's asked as an honest and agonized question, though sometimes it's a way of meaning "We shouldn't trust Muslims" without actually having to say something so un-PC aloud. My answer is that those attentive to Muslim news sources will hear such responses, but not many of us attend to such sources.

So Islam is of interest to us. The problem is that Islam is of interest in the same way as Samuel Huntington's provocative if flawed "clash of civilizations" thesis (which has been popularly reduced to the argument that world politics in the twenty-first century will be shaped by a conflict between the "Islamic" civilization and Western universalism). We're less interested in understanding Islam, the world religion, than in knowing how the political actions of nominal Muslims are likely to affect us. We think politically and call it religious exploration.

From such a starting point, the impact of religious faith on world events may hold our attention in a way that an exploration of religious faith doesn't. That's too bad, since a bit of exploration may mitigate our baser instincts in evaluating religion's impact, if only by adding a bit of clarity to the murky relationship between faith and world events.

But if you want to explore Islam, you might look at "A Common Word," available at www.acommonword.com, which manages to be authentically Islamic in thought and fairly accessible to non-Muslims at the same time. And that makes it an uncommon word.

Debating Health Care

(Appeared February 4, 2007)

The new health care debates are coming, and they're likely to be the most heated debates since the Clintons' plan foundered in 1994. Democratic control of congress plus proactive measures by Republican governors like Mitt Romney and Arnold Schwarzenegger plus President Bush making health insurance tax deductions one of the very few concrete proposals to last week's State of the Union Address (plus increasing health care costs, an increasing percentage of GNP being spent on healthcare, and 48 million Americans who lack health insurance) all but guarantees it.

As the debates grow in intensity, they're likely to generate more heat than light—or so, at least, the evidence of previous debates would suggest. As such, it will be helpful to have a lexicon of rhetorical bogeymen available. When you hear one of the following phrases uttered—whether as promise or threat—be suspicious. And if you hear anyone stringing these phrases together instead of making an argument, it might be better to look for wisdom elsewhere.

Universal health care. Uttered as threat or promise about what might be depending on who's talking, the phrase ignores the fact that we already have a sort of universal health care. As evidence for this, spend a couple days in just about any Emergency Room. As a rule, you're almost certain to be treated whether your means of payment are clear or not. And the exceptions here (people being turned away or getting dumped at other health care facilities) ignite the type of public outrage that only proves the rule. However, we do not have the type of universal health care that covers the wide range of health concerns people face (many of which don't enter medicine through the doors of the ER) or that offers people with similar health problems similar treatment. ER-delivered health care also tends to be expensive and people who rely on the ER for health care tend to wait longer (making their health concern worse) than others, making such care fiscally inefficient as well.

Socialized medicine. This phrase is usually uttered as a threat and ignores (a) the fact that the vast majority of people in most countries with some form of socialized medical care—which includes most Western countries—prefer it; (b) that since health care is a different kind of good than most others we

seek in life, it's quite possible to have a socialized medical system without being a socialist state; and, (c) that we already have a kind of socialized medical system at work. Look over your employer-provided health care plan (if you have one): are there restrictions on who you visit? The types of procedures or medicines it will cover? Who can be in the plan? If there are, you're in a kind of socialized medicine—albeit one more likely to send money through a corporation than the government (Medicaid and Medicare excepted). What we do not have is a fiscally responsible form of socialized medicine.

Tax deductions. Some tax deductions may help in some situations and shouldn't be rejected out of hand. They can't be the basis for a transparent and equitable health care system, though. The notion that tax deductions can help the tens of millions of poor who can't afford personal health insurance and pay very little in taxes, though, is nonsense. And in the absence of some fairly stringent regulations about whom insurance companies must cover, how they must be covered, and how this particular third-party payer method will control costs, a scheme that is premised on the belief that people are better off leaving employer-based insurance to seek out private insurance in order to gain full benefit of the tax deduction is nonsense on stilts. It is one thing to comparison shop for a product you actually need; it's quite another to comparison shop for an almost infinitely wide range of products you may or may not need in the future among insurance companies who, even when acting transparently, can only offer very complex options in the first place.

Malpractice costs. In a litigious society, costs associated with malpractice insurance and lawsuits are, indeed, a problem that needs to be addressed. However, it's a problem that is separable from the current health care crisis. Malpractice awards account for only a very small percentage of the growing costs of health care. As baby-boomers age and technology and treatment grow more sophisticated, health care costs are going to continue to grow regardless of malpractice costs. So if you hear someone bring up malpractice costs in the context of health care costs, turn your ears elsewhere.

Typical liberal (or conservative) responses. There aren't any typical responses to the health care crisis. Some conservatives have offered progressive plans for reform and

some liberals are wedded to current systems. Because of the anomalous way we understand the good of health, health care—more than perhaps any other political concern—defies easy left/right categories.

Whatever direction health care in the U.S. turns as we seek to address its increasingly evident flaws, we're in for some tendentious and frustrating times ahead. We ought not get lost in a fog of false arguments if we're actually interested in the goal of more equitable, effective, and fiscally responsible care, though. Personally, I think the '93 plan needs closer and fairer review—but that's for another column at another time.

Still Debating Health Care
(Appeared July 8, 2007)

Several months ago, I tried to clear out some of the rhetorical underbrush that obstructs helpful debates about health care in the United States. I'm not sure it helped, as that particular column was greeted with both greater acclaim and more vitriol than anything else I've thus far written. But since the debut of Michael Moore's "Sicko" is likely to create more underbrush and greater vitriol, I thought I'd try to do some more clearing. So here is a continuation of that earlier list of phrases used as bogeymen to scare us or ciphers meant to stand in for arguments rather than develop them.

Rationing. Fear of rationing is the great threat raised by those who fear any health plan that can be related in any way to the health care plans of countries in the rest of the Western world, especially Canada and Britain. "If we adopt universal health coverage," the threat goes, "we'll end up stuck in long waiting lines for supplies that aren't currently scarce but will become so because the government will ration them out." Setting aside the fact that many of the same people who use rationing as a threat also look back on the way supplies were rationed

during World War II with a kind of misty-eyed nostalgia for a time when everyone made sacrifices for the good of the whole, this rationing-as-threat argument utterly ignores the fact that our current health care system rations all the time. Sometimes, it rations because resources are scarce (e.g., organs for transplantation). Usually, it rations because insurance companies determine how much care anyone can get in their coverage and people stop going when the insurance company stops paying. And all the time, it rations out health care to those who can afford it, thereby excluding tens of millions of U.S. citizens who lack insurance. The question isn't whether or not health care will be rationed out or not; that's a given. The question is whether there are more just ways of rationing out health care.

Socialized medicine is failing in other countries. What counts as failing? Health indicators like infant mortality, longevity, immunization rates, and disability adjusted life expectancy scores suggest that many countries with "socialized medicine" are doing better than the U.S. Satisfaction levels among the population would suggest that the French system—the *French* system for Pete's sake!—is among the best in the world and almost all other countries are better off than us. Economically, we spend a greater percentage of GNP on health care than other countries, so it's hard to imagine their delivery systems are less efficient than ours (actually, it's hard to figure out what metric to use even to compare efficiency across such different systems). And for every anecdotal example of things falling apart in Canada, Great Britain, or Sweden, there's another example of things working well in Germany, Japan, or Switzerland.

Socialized systems cannot work in the United States. Tell that to the U.S. Military.

The problems with health care delivery can be solved via the free market just like the problems with other delivery systems. This assumes that health is a good like other goods. For a variety of reasons, it isn't. Instead, health is a mix of biological, sociological, and political factors all bound up in a great ball of chance. So, first, though bad health luck is more likely to strike some than others, it always includes a significant degree of arbitrariness. Second, the ability to either recover from or adjust to bad health luck also is something that is partly but never wholly within our control. As a result, try as we might, we cannot

make rational assessments about our health futures with the kind of confidence that we presume to use in making other market decisions. Third, health is a different kind of good because its presence or absence has the possibility of affecting so many other goods. And, fourth, health is a different kind of good because it is incommensurable with other goods; health simply isn't fungible. But if health isn't a good like other goods, it follows that we ought not think that delivery systems that work for other goods will work for health care delivery.

The problems with health care delivery cannot be solved via the free market. Just because the free market isn't a silver bullet, that doesn't mean that it cannot play a role in addressing health care delivery problems. Health isn't unlike other goods because it is wholly arbitrary; it's unlike other goods because it is neither wholly arbitrary nor wholly unpredictable. Some health issues can be addressed by being careful, being active, and being wise. And certainly those matters that can be dealt with in predictable ways admit to some degree of address by the rationality of the market.

The list could go on. In fact, it probably will as the presidential candidates continue to roll out their health plans. But that can wait another few months. In the meantime, I can hardly wait for the praise and condemnation that follows this part of the list.

Dangled Mirages

(Appeared May 27, 2007)

The past few weeks, I've been describing a form of fundamentalism—democratic fundamentalism—at work in American politics. Democratic fundamentalists believe that electing the right person into office will resolve current problems in American political life and that the right person can be discerned by a particular set of personal virtues and cultural dispositions. They favor centralized authority over agonistic politics, moral clarity over social complexity, and righteousness over the rough give-and-take of justice. Democratic fundamentalism allows for Presidential signing statements, illegal domestic surveillance, torturing enemy combatants, and hiring and firing justice department officials on partisan bases. And the primary reason this kind of fundamentalism is linked to the current Republican party is that they're the ones who have been in charge. Were FDR or LBJ's Democratic party in charge, it could as easily have been an expression of their party's politics. To be clear: this isn't about the failings of a particular political party. It's about a culture that has developed a taste for thinking of democracy in terms of leadership rather than rule of law.

The clearest manifestation of this fundamentalism's hold on the American imagination is the degree to which we treat the existence of elections as the primary indicator of functioning democracies. States are moving their primaries earlier and earlier in order to shape impending elections. Debates between candidates are already well underway. And political pundits promote the ineffable quality of "leadership" as vital to winning elections: Rudy can win the presidency on its basis; Hillary can't.

Elections are necessary but insufficient. Functioning democracies require rule of law as well as elections. That's why the presidential oath of office isn't about promoting a particular vision of the common good, uniting the country, or shaping a political trajectory for the future. It's an oath to "preserve, protect and defend the Constitution of the United States." And, as interpreters of that document know, the actual functions designated to the President are relatively limited in comparison to those given to the legislature—principally serving as Commander in Chief, giving State of the Union addresses in which he makes recommendations to the

legislature, appointing ambassadors and Supreme Court Justices (but only with Senate consent), and seeing that "the Laws be faithfully executed." The Founding Fathers were as interested in constraining the powers of the presidency as we are in extending them.

The occasion of Jerry Falwell's death is helpful in making sense of this fundamentalism. Falwell, for all his failings, believed in elections. He also believed in a strong America—albeit according to a troublingly idiosyncratic version thereof. He believed in the presidency—so much so that he was willing to forgo his earlier resistance to Christian involvement in politics in order to make sure that Reagan was elected. He even believed in democracy. What he didn't believe in was rule of law, because rule of law is what you get once you surrender the notions that justice is neat, that we can get things right once and for all, and that the majority—whether moral or not—should be able to say how other people live. It isn't that Falwell brought fundamentalism into politics; it's that a particular form of political fundamentalism brought Falwell into power. So neither his death nor the decline of the Christian right is going to fix what ails us. Since politics tends to follow culture rather than vice-versa, recovering from democratic fundamentalism will, instead, require nurturing an alternative cultural vision of democracy.

Among the most captivating expressions of that vision was one laid out a century and a half ago by Walt Whitman in his poem, "To a President":

All you are doing and saying is to
America dangled mirages,
You have not learn'd of Nature—of
the politics of Nature you
have not learn'd the great
amplitude, rectitude,
impartiality,
You have not seen that only such as
they are for these States,
And that what is less than they
must sooner or later lift off
from these States.

It is the "amplitude, rectitude, and impartiality" of the American people, not the "dangled mirages" of Presidential ambition that are the basis of American democratic society. It can't be about getting the right leader in place; it can only be about citizens living into a vision of political nature that is generous, moral, and fair. So as you listen to the buzzing of candidates over the next year and a half, remember two things: First, democracy survives where authority is dispersed and the rule of law is promoted. And second, its success turns on how we think about ourselves, not what we think about them.

Stuck in the Muddle Again

(January 14, 2007)

The 110th Congress is now in session, replacing the mercifully departed 109th Congress, which set records for its lack of work. Hopes are high in some quarters (notably newly cheery democratic ones) that this congressional season will be an improvement on the last one: more days at work, more oversight of the Executive Branch (it is in the job description, after all), more bills brought to completion, and, if not more bipartisanship, at least fewer rule-by-cabal tactics. May it be so.

But those whose hopes ride high with the new Congress may be in for a year of disappointments—and not only because a narrowly Democratic Senate and House will still have to contend with a Republican White House. Nor, for that matter, because it turns out that Democrats in charge are no more virtuous than Republicans—though after a scandal-ridden 2006, it's hard to imagine how they could be less virtuous. Instead, disappointments may be the product of the changing face of democracy in the U.S.

Conventional wisdom has highlighted the way American government pendulums between constitutional democracy and populist democracy. If the "swinging pendulum" theory is correct, then constitutional democracy, marked by its focus on representational government, checks-and-balances, rule of law, and the affirmation of certain basic rights for citizens—even where those rights apply most clearly to an unpopular minority—would seem to be on the wane. Between the theory of the unitary executive, NSA wiretaps on U.S. citizens, the practices of extraordinary rendition and torture, and Congress' tendency to fund the government by continuing resolution rather than debated appropriations bills, one wonders that we've not been haunted by the ghosts of angry founding fathers.

Populist democracy, on the other hand, certainly seems to be surging. Rule-by-popular sentiment (constitutional marriage amendments, hand-wringing over Iraq, mindless and often malicious proposals about immigration, etc.), a preoccupation with symbols (Terri Schiavo, soldiers, and a ban on flag-burning), replacing the activities of patriotism with the passions of nationalism (I'd bet more people have "Support Our Troops" stickers on their cars than voted in the last election), the theatrics of faux-common-men like Lou Dobbs and Bill O'Reilly and the demagoguery-lite of John Edwards, Sam Brownback, and, yes, Barack Obama, all point toward populism as the political direction of the day.

The turn toward populist democracy is hardly surprising. What else would we expect with the baby-boomers politically ascendant? They are, after all, the magnificently self-absorbed generation that bought into the "don't trust authority" patter of the New Left in the '60s and the "government is the problem" claims of the new right in the '80s. The kind of populism that empowered and then deserted the 109th Congress is a force of contemporary culture.

More surprising, though, is that the seeming decline of constitutional democracy may not be a real decline. The trajectory of the Roberts Supreme Court suggests that its rulings are more likely to be conservative in the sense that they attend to nuances of current law than in the sense that they will be welcomed by social conservatives. The theory of the unitary executive never needed to get put into practice while the legislature rolled over for the president and isn't likely to be tried in the face of the new Congress. Minds are changing about extending the rights of marriage (if not its titles) to gays and

lesbians. It's too early to tell what the new Congress will do with regard to either immigration or the more legally troubling aspects of the Patriot Act and the war on terror. And regardless of what some social conservatives might think, it remains highly unlikely that a precedent-setting ruling like *Roe v. Wade* will be overturned.

So what might it mean that constitutional democracy and populist democracy may be growing simultaneously? Have our political divisions reached the point of schizophrenia? Is the growth of populism a sign of just how settled the vast majority of us are with the Constitution—it being both easier and more interesting to debate symbols and appeal to emotions than to shape real change? Has government become too big to run on anything other than representation, bureaucracy, and rule of law at the same time that citizens have become too ignorant to understand any form of democracy other than populism? And what role do the changing functions of the media and political parties play in all this?

It is probably too early to answer those questions, though the actions of the 110th Congress—not to mention the social impetuses for those actions and public responses to them—may give us some hints, so it will be worth watching it closely. John Dewey famously claimed that the solution to the problems of democracy was more democracy. If only we knew which kinds of democracy were the problems and which were the solutions.

4 Love and Public Life

There are any number of ways to participate in public life: voting, campaigning, picking up litter, paying taxes, having block parties, attaching magnetic yellow "ribbons" that read "support our troops" to the back of one's car, buying American/organic/local, etc. For a year and a half, the two ways I most consciously participated in public life were these: I wrote editorials and I went to church. Hopefully at this point in the book, readers have given up on the notion—if they ever had it—that going to church is a "private" thing.

In chapter 2, I lined out some of the reasons I wrote editorials. I went to church for a variety of reasons as well. To see friends. To fulfill a sense of obligation pressed upon me since my youth. To nurture the spiritual development of my daughter. For the bagels and donuts during fellowship hour. To maintain marital bliss. (My wife was the senior pastor of the church I attended.) Above all, though, I went for two reasons. First, I went to gather with people who do not think like I do about political matters. Second—and more importantly—I went to be reminded that I am loved.

Take those two reasons in order. I doubt there is any context in which people with more varied political perspectives gather, sit with each other, and call each other "friend" than in mainline churches on Sunday mornings. Or at least any context in which people feel both an obligation to get along with each other and the freedom to share their thoughts.

Undoubtedly, the church—and mainline churches perhaps in particular—have miles to go before the range of pew-sitters is as broad (politically, racial-ethnically, spiritually) as the broader population. But then so do other places where people gather and, while the failings of other communities hardly excuse those of the church, at least most mainline churches I know see those failings as failings and are working for change.

At church, I can gather with a community of believers and half-believers, like-minded and not-so-like minded, visionaries and keepers of memories—pilgrims all—for support, for challenge, for company, and for wisdom. And I needed that diverse group of people and their gifts in an especially acute way while writing editorials on public issues.

In my experience, editorial writers face twin temptations. The first is to claim that they understand what is going on better than anyone else. They write to explain, to teach, to ridicule. Such editorial writers—on both the left and the right—assume that their theories and their ideologies are adequate to every situation; they lay their vision over the top of whatever issue they are discussing and then either ignore or cut off whatever parts of the world don't fit. In the process, they tend to either ignore or cut off those whose visions differ from their own. The first temptation, then, is to explain the world too well—to explain it with greater clarity than the world actually admits. I think I caved in to this temptation in my article "Tortured Logic,"* partly because I wrote on a topic (the use of torture) about which I have trouble seeing any legitimacy in other perspectives. My goal should have been to express my own strongly held opinion without precluding hearing others' opinions as a way of shaping a better conversation with them and, thereby, hopefully changing their minds rather than damning their thoughts.

The second temptation is to surrender to the complexity of the world. Editorialists who submit to the second temptation write to complicate, to frustrate, to prognosticate. They pick apart other people's arguments but remain mute when asked to offer their own solutions. Such editorial writers—again, on both the left and the right—see through the theories and ideologies of others and bemoan the consequences of pursuing agendas based on those theories and ideologies. Yet while reminders about our own finitude and the limitations of our visions are helpful, in themselves they don't move conversations forward, usually at the very time we most desperately need forward movement. The second temptation is to say the world is inexplicable—to assume that if we cannot understand it, it cannot be understood. I think I caved in to this temptation in my article, "Childhood Fetish,"* which, looked back upon a year later, seemed full of criticism (and, sadly, criticism of the most generalized sort) without offering anything substantial of my own. My goal in that column should have been to advance an argument about why children matter in our society rather than just mocking what I take to be failed arguments about their significance—to place a discrete and concrete idea in front of people rather than just lob conceptual hand grenades from nowhere in particular.

Part of what made these temptations enticing is that I often fought each of them in the process of writing a single editorial: I fought—not always successfully—the second temptation *while* writing most of my editorials. I imagine most writers facing a blank page have doubted whether they really have anything to say or if they can successfully say it. This temptation reinforces those doubts in offering a path marked by unremitting criticism taken from a posture of world-worn knowingness. In the face of self-doubt, it's simply easier to maintain your ego if you don't try to put your own arguments in front of people and instead just criticize those of others. And I fought the first temptation—again, not always successfully—after I'd finished many of my editorials and sent them off. Once I'd committed to them (and nothing says commitment like hitting the "Send" button), it was easier to admire my thoughts than examine them.

I imagine these two temptations—to assume too much about the world and to demand too little of ourselves—are confronted by more than editorial writers.

Different as they may seem, the two temptations share important commonalities. Most obviously, both temptations invite us not only to accept the world as it presents itself to us but to submit to the idea that the presented world is all that there is. Left behind are claims—religious and otherwise—that the world is not yet complete, that it is a relatively orderly part of a far larger system, that complexity does not obviate discernment, or that the problems may have more to do with what's in us (e.g., our limited imaginations, our need to take shortcuts along the way to wisdom, our desire to maintain the integrity of our own egos) than what's out there.

Both temptations also share a language problem: neither approach suggests an actual interest in communicating. Communication, after all, involves give and take, talking and listening, sending and receiving. Appearing to participate in public conversation, they actually inhibit it by presuming that theirs is the last word: either "I am right and will brook no dissent" (the first temptation) or "There is nothing to say other than that you are wrong." (the second).

And both temptations convey a sense that we are the only ones who can address the problems and complexities of the world. The first temptation invites us to think of ourselves as alone and capable of addressing them; the second to think that because we cannot fully address them, they cannot be addressed. Both are products of a kind of self-absorption.

By way of further evidence for all this, consider the growing blogosphere. While there are many thoughtful blogs on the web, the relative absence of outside editors asking questions about whether blog material is worth publishing or reading lends an air of egocentrism to many blogs. Even those blogs by established authors, scholars, newspersons, and other celebrities—many of which are connected to mainstream media establishments—tend to be written in a more casual and personality-driven style that further blurs the line between insightful reflection and vanity publishing. I'm hardly innocent in all this. Not only did I link my Facebook page (which is, after all, all about me) to the editorial section of the online edition of *The Sunday Paper*—so that my Facebook friends could read what I wrote—but I Facebooked about the editorials I wrote, including suggesting that I treated my editorials as a blog for which I got paid.

Undoubtedly, the power of the Web to extend the range of conversations to include more participants can pay significant benefits and blogs may play an important role in this. At this point, though, the web doesn't necessarily extend the depth of those conversations, partly because it makes it easier only to read the thoughts of people with whom one agrees. As a result, vanity reinforces vanity: reader and writer form a shrinking society of self-admiration. The quality of public conversation is diminished even as the number of people involved in such a quasi-public conversation grows.

What has going to church to do with this? At least this: going to church meant entering a venue in which my self-absorption—encouraged though it was by writing editorials—could be challenged without leaving me deflated. Partly this was because of the people I encountered there. As I noted, I can think of no setting in which more people of differing political and cultural convictions gather on a regular basis and willingly talk with each other (and share pews and meals with each other) than contemporary mainline churches. So when I went to church, I talked with people who do not think like me or see the world the way I see it. And partly this was because at church I had my perspective enlarged in such a way that I was reminded both that I mattered and that I was not the center of the universe. As if being a finalist for a national award for editorial writing and being let go as an editorial writer within a few months of each other weren't evidence enough of that!

I doubt, though, that I would continue to go to church if that were my primary reason for attending. The primary reason I went was to be reminded that I am loved.

Perhaps that sounds cliché or romantic or saccharine or self-absorbed. I don't mean it to. I mean that fundamental to the Christian vision of life in the world is the conviction that we (and the world) are created, sustained, and being transformed by the love of a gracious God and that this love not only makes our own actions possible but orients those actions toward their proper ends: love of God and love of neighbor. To be reminded of that, I went to church.

At church, I can find weekly—sometimes daily—reminders that we haven't been left to our own devices and that this is not as good as it gets. I can get help in seeing God at work in the world and seeing the world as a place that God has chosen to work. I can talk with others and discover that the world and its issues are too complex and mysterious for me to think that my ideas and ideologies are adequate to exhaustively describe what is going on—but that in spite of that complexity and mysteriousness (or, rather, in light of it and my desire to describe it), something new is happening in it. It is love—above all, before all, through all—that shapes a Christian vision of God's work in the world and motivates a Christian response to the world. That vision and response have always been shaped by the larger community of believers, namely, the church.

Yet what does this love look like? And how does it meaningfully engage public matters? These are the key questions of this chapter.

The Shape of Christian Love

Many kinds of love form communities. Families, neighborhoods, civic organizations, schools, nations, etc: all of them are shaped by the bonds of love and all of them, in their existence and habits, reveal the kinds of love that form them. St. Augustine went so far as to suggest that a community is any collection of persons who agree about what they love. Christians, as a community (i.e., the church), are the collection of persons who agree that they are commanded and enabled to love God and neighbor. How, though, do Christians do this?

As a start, we remember two things: First, God is the source of all love and human identity is founded in this love. Second, because we do not yet love as God loves (because we do not yet see as God sees), we must remember that we are in the process of learning to love as God loves by learning to see as God sees.

Begin with the first claim: that God is the source of all love and human identity is founded in this love. For human beings, there is both threat and promise in the claim that our identity is founded in God's love. We feel this claim as threat because it means to see who we are we must look beyond ourselves. We feel it as threat because we are always dependent upon something beyond ourselves and, therein, vulnerable to another: the very thing that most makes us *us* is something that isn't uniquely ours. Fearing that vulnerability, we seek to found ourselves in something that can be uniquely our own: choice, rationality, our genes, or some other basic and intrinsically human category. We envision ourselves as separable from God and, by continually envisioning ourselves as separated from God, we offer up descriptions that separate our identity from the One who loves us and makes us love.

Then, seeking a description of ourselves that can fill the hole left by absenting God's love from our identity, we love wrongly. Believing that if we don't love ourselves, nobody else will, we focus on ourselves (and pride becomes a kind of compensation for our failure to believe that we are loved). Believing that we aren't worthy of love, we undervalue ourselves (and self-abnegation becomes compensation for our failure to recognize that in being loved we are valued). Believing that we will be more loved by a community, we submerge ourselves into that community's vision of life (and so finite and faulty communities become compensations for our failure to see that only God's love can complete us).

We reinforce these compensations—and find them so convincing— because we bombard ourselves and each other with the very messages that promote such bad descriptions. Hoping to raise self-reliant children, parents teach their kids to "look out for number one," while ignoring the contradiction that good parenting is premised on a human willingness to surrender years, material, and sometimes life itself in order to look out for another. Or tiring of so much surrender, parents teach children—usually implicitly—that they aren't worth all the time and trouble that come with raising children. Religious leaders and advertising jingles simultaneously stroke our egos by telling us of our importance and convince us that we are incomplete without the truth they hold and the products they hawk. Politicians tell us that they're fighting for things we hold dear while withholding the fact that life in civil society necessarily means surrendering some things we value in order to maintain others. And so on . . .

Worse, in rejecting a vision of ourselves that turns on being unequivocally loved by God, we also reject a vision of others that turns on that same source of value. Unable to see ourselves principally as loved, we are unable to see others in that way and, as a result, we fail to love them—just as they, fearing the same vulnerability and pursuing the same reinforcements against it, fail to love us.

Thus are we spun in a vicious cycle: fearing vulnerability, we stand against God and our neighbors, but in taking such a stand, we make ourselves vulnerable to bad interpretations of ourselves and to malicious forces that spring out of and benefit from such interpretations. As we then feel more vulnerable to such interpretations and forces, we become more fearful of our own essential vulnerability. Trapped in this vicious cycle, we cannot distinguish between the essential vulnerability that comes from our identity being dependent upon God and the many vulnerabilities we have shaped in trying to escape that essential vulnerability. Ironically, it isn't so much our vulnerability as our failure to accept being vulnerable that makes us helpless.

Fundamentalisms—whether associated with particular religions or not—are attempts to avoid vulnerability by trying to base our thoughts and/or beliefs in someone or something that we wish to see as invulnerable. Against our essential vulnerability, fundamentalist projects are ultimately doomed. Between now and their downfall, though, they are both inviting and destructive—a point I tried not-very-successfully to make in "A New Fundamentalism,"* which was received more with headscratching than agreement or disagreement. I think most readers thought of fundamentalism as an essentially religious term, so to use it in any other way created more dissonance than my attempt at explanation was able to relieve.

Our essential vulnerability, however, isn't like other vulnerabilities. It isn't like the vulnerability founded on insecurities about technological complexity, political ambiguity, economic uncertainty, or religious perplexity. Instead, the vulnerability of human identity founded in God's love is one that is shaped by security. We are held too fast, our lives too revealed, our hopes too formed to accord with our own badly-shaped desires. We are loved too much and too insistently by God for this identity ever to be at risk. We cannot build ramparts against the vulnerability at the heart of human identity precisely because such vulnerability is the foundation of that identity. Attempting to do so makes no more sense than trying to become what we are not in order to ensure that we can remain what we are. We literally *are* vulnerable because we are loved by God.

So even in the helpless whirl of confused vulnerabilities, there is the hint of our salvation. Yes, we are unable to make ourselves invulnerable. But because we are unable to make ourselves invulnerable, we cannot but remain open to the workings of the one who can redeem us from our partial and failing attempts to be invulnerable. Because we are vulnerable, we are vulnerable to God. So while on the one hand we cannot redeem ourselves, on the other we need not think that we must do so: the one who can redeem us is the one who has made us and continues to shape us into the ones God is turning us into.

The claim that our identity simply is being loved by God holds a promise that is deeper than threat. Because our identity is defined by God's love, that identity is encompassed and redeemed by God. Our identity isn't bound up in just anything that is beyond ourselves but is instead tied to the One whose permanence and goodness mean that we can never be divorced from that identity. Nothing can separate us from who we are because nothing can separate us from the one whose claim on us makes us.

This vision of vulnerability and value then shapes the way we pick up the second claim: that since we do not yet love as God loves (because we do not see as God sees), learning to love involves learning to see as God sees.

Take the examples of two very different columns I wrote: "Soldiers and Saints"* and "The Indignant and the Indigent."* Both columns were about a social failure to see others as God sees them: as human beings who, too, have not yet made sense of what it means to be loved by God. The former column speaks for itself. The latter may need a bit more explanation. I wrote that column because a colleague of mine who had spent years working with the state of Georgia to develop a just and politically feasible way to try those who could not afford attorneys was watching his efforts come undone. Some politicians were taking advantage of a high-profile murder case in which the defendant shot and killed several people—including a judge and a sheriff—while escaping custody in order to advance their own political careers. The former article was received mostly with goodwill and gratitude (and several returning veterans with whom I talked spoke warmly of it). The latter attracted more diverse opinions—some commendatory and some openly hostile. Defending soldiers is easy compared to defending those accused of crimes (especially those who already lack social status). Loving either of them as humans, though, is difficult.

To see better how learning to love involves learning to see (God at work in the world, others as neighbors loved by God, the world as God's creation . . .), I want to suggest that love does two things in shaping our vision. First, it cultivates our discontentments. Second, it challenges our fears. Each of those warrants its own sub-section. Then, enriched by those sections, we'll return, albeit too briefly, to the questions of sight and love at the end of this chapter.

Cultivating Our Discontentments

If one thinks of love as something that brings serenity and peace—the kind of "la da da da da" feeling that comes in the chorus of the Beatles' song, "All You Need Is Love"—the idea that love cultivates discontentment will undoubtedly be counterintuitive. Shouldn't love replace or remove our various discontentments? Well, yes—and no. Undoubtedly, many of the things that make us discontent are driven as much by the feeling of love's absence as anything else (think, for example, of the dissatisfaction in a marriage between two people who have fallen out of love with each other). Love's presence may have the effect of driving discontentment away; where this happens, I think the process reveals in a fitful and partial way the degree to which love and fulfillment are ultimately bound up in each other. At the end of the day, love is discontent with discontentment. We are not yet at the end of the day, though—or, rather, we are not yet at its bright beginning—and until then discontentment and love's discontent with it signals something too complex to be summed up in the simple equation of love with serenity.

So what does love's discontent signal? While it may signal the promise that ultimately fulfillment will replace discontentment, there is more to love than promise. And this side of eternity, at least to judge from all available data, discontentment is an inevitable part of life. Such discontentment points not only to our failings (which love may ameliorate) but to our incompleteness—to the need for change, for growth, for progress. And, I think, it points to an inchoate awareness that there is something deeper, something more good and true and beautiful than we have yet found. Until we are complete, we will be discontent.

The question, then, is what to do with our various discontentments? Denying them seems fruitless, ignoring them naïve, and submitting ourselves to their whims destructive. Perhaps, instead, we should cultivate them much as a farmer cultivates his crops, seeking to remove weeds and weak plants, prune stronger ones and nourish and water them until they are ripe. Of the many things we can use to cultivate discontentment (hate, envy, insecurity, etc.), love is among the most provocative and meaningful tools we have and the only one among them that Christians receive as both a blessing and a command.

How, though, does love cultivate our discontentments? In several ways, not least of which is, as I've begun to suggest above, by giving them a place in our lives as a way of reminding us that we are becoming something that we are not yet. In the process of moving from where we are to what we are being made into, we will almost certainly be called upon to surrender certain things that we currently enjoy in order to participate in greater joys (a process that the church has long named "asceticism"—a word that unfortunately now conjures up images of starving wild-haired hermits rejecting sex and comfort rather than the far-more-common projects of self-discipline that we might associate with athletes in training, recovering addicts in 12-step programs, or students taking challenging courses). Even more likely, we'll be encouraged to learn to love things we may not currently like and to love things we already love in new ways: family members become neighbors, careers become vocations, love of country becomes civic responsibility.

As love cultivates our discontentments, we learn more about loving God. We learn about the idols we worship instead of God by noticing how discontent our worship of them makes us. We learn about the limits of our language by noticing how discontent the stories we tell and the arguments we make concerning our pasts, present, and future leave us. We even learn that our discontentment with our discontentments about idol-worship and language may point us toward God rather than simply away from things that are not God. We do all of this by continually asking ourselves, "Who or what am I loving when I love this thing/this story/ this argument?" Along the way, we discover—almost as if by accident— something about a divine love that permits and shapes our questions, our learning, and our love: because God loves us in ways beyond our understanding, we learn to love God through processes that change our understanding.

I tried to explore this idea of discontentment and openendedness (though in a less theologically developed way) in "Making Ourselves at Home,"* an editorial that laid groundwork for a series of columns I wrote over the course of several weeks. The editorials that followed it explored the narratives that the various presidential candidates of 2008 were telling about what America was like. Betraying my own (now obvious) biases toward abstract thought—something I may have to learn to love differently (though not quite yet!), I'll admit that "Making Ourselves at Home" was the editorial in the series that I most enjoyed writing because in it I was trying to think out a new idea—and this even though the later columns garnered more responses. The subsequent columns were mostly about testing my big idea against the candidates' speeches; as such, they felt more mechanical and therefore less likely to grow any new ideas. Perhaps this reveals nothing more than the dangers of getting too attached to— of falling too much in love with—a new idea. I'd like to think, though, that my frustration with the columns that followed had more to do with the word-limit: trying to work out the big idea meant less of a chance to develop any new ideas.

Just as love cultivates our discontentments in order to better love God, so love cultivates our discontentments in order for us to better love our neighbors. We learn about the prejudices we carry against others by noticing how discontent we are with a world filled with prejudice. We learn about the limits of the language we use to talk to others by noticing how discontent we are when they use the same language to talk to us. We learn about the limits of antagonism when we notice how discontent we are with a vision of a world structured by antagonisms. We do all this by continually asking ourselves, "If this is someone God loves, why am I having so much trouble loving her?" And along the way, we discover— perhaps less accidentally—that learning to love someone because he is loved by God is too difficult to do if we're left to our own devices: because

God loves us in spite of our understandings of others, we can learn to love others.

The process of learning to cultivate discontentment is not easy. Indeed, this discontentment is one of the primary reasons that the ways we learn to love our neighbors—forgiving them and being forgiven by them, seeking justice for them without losing sight of the goal of reconciliation, being hospitable to those we do not know without minimizing the significance of time spent with those we do—feel so consistently difficult, regularly dissatisfying, persistently temporary, and repeatedly contradictory. While forgiveness, justice, reconciliation, and hospitality are all expressions of divine love, our halting and partial expressions of them leave us wanting more. That is, even when we think we're trying to do them right, they leave us discontent and with questions about whether it's worth it to pursue this whole neighbor-love thing and, if so, how to do it correctly (to which I suppose one fairly inadequate response is to ask whether *not* going about pursuing forgiveness, justice, etc., would be any more likely to lead to contentment). The road to hell may be paved with good intentions but it is also littered with the frustrations of those who tried to do the right thing only to watch their problems grow as a result.

At least for anyone trying to speak religiously in the public sphere of a democracy (that is, anyone trying to believe aloud in a political context that emphasizes conversation), these frustrations regularly form around how we talk with each other. From those who have found shouting more effective than talking to those who use language not so much to describe the world around them as to conceal what they're doing from others; from those who feel trapped by either the fear of offending someone or the threat of being criticized for using words that cause pain to those who use words to cause pain: language is both the primary means by which we move forward and among the most likely things that keep us from doing so.

Making matters worse, our attempts to improve how we talk (or, more likely, how other people talk) can exacerbate the very problems we're trying to overcome. And because talking is such an important part of our lives together and so fraught with risk, we're especially preoccupied by it. I wrote "Hocus Pocus"* as a way of picking up on some of these concerns. Written immediately after shock-jock Don Imus was fired for comments he made about the Rutgers University women's basketball team, I was trying to highlight the irony of empowering others by identifying them as victims while—as I hoped would be clear—trying to treat both the basketball team and Imus as my neighbors. While I certainly didn't condone Imus's remarks, I thought firing him was a counterproductive response. It was the only editorial that my editor chose not to publish.

When my editor told me she wouldn't run the column, I showed it to several colleagues (including women and African Americans) to see if they found it deficient. Though all of them were respectful and friendly, several of them disagreed with me, arguing that some things simply should not be said and Imus's remarks justified his firing, which could serve as an example for those who would use language so unthoughtfully and uncharitably. These are very intelligent people for whom I have enormous amounts of respect. Here's the thing, though: try as I might, I simply couldn't understand their reasoning (or, rather, what I did understand of it I didn't find compelling). They seemed to be expressing the same frustrations with me. And these were conversations with friends who also use words professionally, many of them far more beautifully than I do! If we couldn't get our conversation right, how can strangers without as much training in the uses and abuses of words get their conversations right? The question is maddening but reveals the degree to which discontentment pervades life.

There are any number of insights I can take away from those events: I still have a great deal to learn about the way race works in American society. The power of words is far more subtle than I give it credit for. Well-meaning thoughtful people can not only disagree, they can fail to even achieve a level of disagreement as they talk past each other. For the purpose of this chapter, though, the points to take away from all this are: (a) that my discontentment with the way words are used reveals my need to continue to cultivate that discontentment; (b) that I need to continue to learn to love better as a way of cultivating those discontentments; and (c) believing aloud is going to challenge anyone who attempts to cultivate their discontentments with love.

The point I hope not to take away from these events, though, is that we should be afraid of believing aloud, of being discontent, or of being changed as a result of making those discontentments audible as we attempt to believe aloud. To explore this point in greater detail, I turn to the other focal point of this chapter: how love challenges fear.

Perfect Love Casts Out Fear.

Writing after 9/11, during two wars, and in the midst of cultural and political upheaval meant writing into a U.S. context in which fear played a major role. The news media—of which I was, for a while, a part—responded to, fed on, and regularly exacerbated that fear. I read a fair number of Chicken Little editorials warning of falling skies. The range of threatened catastrophes we faced—global temperatures at a tipping point, terrorism at our doorstep and unguarded nukes god-knows-where, the wrong person elected President or the wrong party in charge of Congress, China owning too much U.S. debt and health care costs spinning out of control, the traditional family falling apart, etc.—sometimes left me wondering where I could find a hole to crawl into.

I also read a fair number of "Everybody Just Calm Down, Now" editorials, assuring us that cooler heads would prevail—to which I regularly wondered "Which heads? And what is their relation to the heads that got us into some of these messes?" Such editorials felt less soothing than disingenuous. Perhaps the skies weren't falling but there were still things falling out of the skies. While the first type of editorial seems irresponsible, the second type seems naïve: panic may misguidedly give too much attention to danger but there are still legitimate and fairly imminent threats out there to deal with.

I wrote "The (Ad)Vantage of Democracy"* partly as a response to the whiplashing movement between being told to panic and being told not to worry. Its point was not to dismiss fear but to orient it. Had I more space, I would have pointed out that modern democracies are not so much the products of our hopes and dreams but our fears: fear of our neighbors leaves us seeking political systems with enough power to protect us from them; fear of the state leaves us seeking limits on those political systems so that states can't take from us things we think are properly ours—our lives and our liberties foremost among them. And I wrote "A Government of the People"* as a reminder to us that too much fear of the state's power—especially the power to tax—can also be destructive.

In both articles, I was trying neither to submit to our fears nor to ignore them, but instead to evaluate and order them. This is no small task when we're afraid. Fear's great weapon, after all, is that it inhibits our ability to deal with it thoughtfully. It encourages reaction rather than response, so when we're afraid, we tend to flee or to fight, thereby making things worse (and in the process exacerbating the causes of our fears). All too many Christian pronouncements on public matters seemed caught up in "fight" mode even as all too many Christian organizations seemed to be in "flight" mode. Neither approach is adequate to a Christian vision in which God is reconciling all things to himself.

For Christians, at least, ordering our fears means trying to place them in larger contexts that recognize our inescapable finitude, our connections to each other (including connections to those that we consider strangers and enemies), our reliance upon God's grace, and the aforementioned vision of God's reconciling work. All of which is to say that though Christians do not escape fear, they give love—and not fear—prominence of place in the way they engage the world and therein evaluate and order their fears based on the integrity of the love they have been created and commanded to give.

This is tricky because fear feeds, parasitically, on love. We do not fear for the welfare of those we do not love. We do not fear the loss of things that we do not care about. Fear, then, reveals what we love and how much we love it. But it does so in a perverse way: by attempting to remove from us our ability to attend to those people and things in coherently loving ways. The fear that a toy will be damaged will prevent a child from the pleasures of using or sharing it. The fear that our sons and daughters will be injured keeps us from teaching them to ride bikes, climb trees, play sports, and otherwise undergo the activities that give them a zest for life and wisdom about the possibilities and limits of their own abilities. The fear that success in difficult projects will only lead to responsibilities beyond our abilities keeps us from taking them on and thereby cuts us off from the sense of satisfaction that comes in a job well done. The fear of lifelong commitment to another person keeps us from marrying (or staying married) and thereby learning about the joys and struggles of sharing our lives with a partner.

It is not enough, then, just to use our fears to signal our priorities or point out our loves because our fears also inhibit our ability to thoughtfully examine our loves. We not only need to be aware of our loves but to question them. And to do so, we need to anchor them in a larger story that teaches about what is worth loving and how to love it. Christians find this anchor in the story of God's creation, redemption, and sustaining of the world. That is to say, the Christian story of God's love helps us orient our own loves and, in the process, gives us the traction with which to oppose, organize, and overcome our fears.

Christian love *opposes* our fears by reminding us that we have not been left to our own devices; that God's promises are not toward destruction but transformation; that though we will still experience things that make us afraid (not the least of which are pain and death), these things do not have the last word; that making our own comfort and security our primary goal is not only a doomed project but one that will most likely have the effect of making us feel less comfortable and secure.

Christian love *organizes* our fears by inviting us to clarify for ourselves what things are most important to us and what things are of passing import; by asking us what standards we use in evaluating their importance; and by calling us to evaluate those standards by reference to the story of what God is doing in and for the world. Along the way, we may discover that some things are not worth being afraid of and some things we fear too much or too little. And along the way, we learn to distinguish between fears we can do something about, fears we must leave for others to do something about, and fears that none of us can do anything about.

And Christian love *overcomes* our fears by anchoring us in a theological vision and a historic community that helps provide us with the kind of conceptual traction we need to challenge and organize our fears. This isn't to say that love leaves Christians fearless; there are, as I have noted, things that warrant our fear. It is, however, to say that Christian love overcomes the immobilizing panic of fear, the reactivity of unreflective fight or flight, and the sense that there is more to fear in the world than to love.

To add concreteness to these claims about how Christian love opposes, organizes, and overcomes our fears, I return to the focus of this book: believing aloud in a U.S. context. In the chapter on faith, I lined out a number of reasons that Christians should engage as Christians in the public sphere. I did not, though, address one of the primary reasons that we do not so engage: we are afraid of doing so. We fear being revealed as a Christian (even in relatively tolerant societies like that of the U.S., behaving in distinctly Christian ways or being vocal about one's faith can have stigmatizing effects). We fear being revealed as an inadequately thoughtful Christian (even the brightest among Christians recognize that we do not have all the answers; indeed, to be Christian is to *assume* that we do not have those answers and that even if we did, we would not be able to pursue them through our own strengths). We fear getting into arguments we can't gracefully get back out of (none of us can predict the effect our words will have on others and on many contentious issues it feels like our words are as likely to inflame debate as add insight). We fear later being revealed as a hypocrite or being forced to maintain a perspective that it grows harder and harder to hold. We fear appearing self-righteous, speaking in public, being asked to put our money where our mouths are, alienating friends, family, or co-workers, etc. There are good reasons to be afraid of believing aloud! And there are some not-so-good reasons as well. So how does Christian love address—oppose, organize, and overcome— these particular fears?

Christian love *opposes* these fears by reminding us that as lonely as we may feel when believing aloud, we aren't alone. For many of us, few things feel more isolating than speaking in front of others—especially when the subject matter is not only personal but something we aren't used to or entirely comfortable talking publicly about. At times, it helped me to remember that scripture and the history of the church are full of people who weren't keen on speaking about their faith but did so anyway (though sometimes after some convincing). Regularly, these people were able to do so because they were reminded that they were not and could not be isolated or hidden anyway. God, who loves them, saw and was present with them. Said differently, the reminder that we are always public—that we always have a public in a loving God—challenges the ideas that we are isolated and that we can avoid feeling isolated by being private.

Moreover, Christian love opposes the fear of being public by re- minding us that we are not being called to give the right response but a faithful one, which helps in two ways. Not only does it unburden us from the feeling that we need to make the results of our actions come out right but it invites us to recognize that faith, as *faith*, is not the same thing as surety. We can only believe those things that we can also doubt; to think otherwise not only misunderstands the structure of believing but the power of belief as well. Whatever else it may mean, then, believing aloud can't mean talking about things we're sure of. We don't pronounce from on high when we speak in public; we *confess* from the midst of that public.

Popular understandings of confession have confused it with litanies of sins. Politicians confess marital infidelity; bankers confess avaricious acts; criminals confess crimes. Theologically speaking, though, confes- sion isn't so much a series of claims about what we have or have not done as a recognition of who we are and where we find ourselves. Confession is more a project in spiritual geography than a kind of ritualized guilt-speech. When we confess sins, it is because we have come to recognize something ugly in the landscape of our lives that needs to be named. By that same token, though, we confess faith as well as sin because we can also recognize the beauty in that landscape. When Christians speak in public settings, we confess because we are simultaneously a part of the public—and therein able to find the beauty in it that warrants our concern—and attentive to something ugly in that public of which we are a part. To allow fear to inhibit our willingness to speak in public is tantamount to ignoring both that which is ugly and that which is beautiful in the public sphere.

Within this posture of confession, Christian love *orders* our fears by asking us first to use them as a way of seeing into our loves and then examining what our fears tell us about our loves. In a kind of mirrored move, our fears reveal our actual loves so we can compare them to what we would most like to love. Then our deeper loves can reveal what isn't worth fearing, what is worth fearing, and how much to fear. Our fears show us the way we have ordered our loves so we can test their quality; our loves can then reveal the significance or insignificance of our fears.

Perhaps one of us is afraid of looking or sounding foolish. What might this tell him about his desire for or love of appearing proper or smart? Perhaps another is afraid of being asked whether she's actually willing to make sacrifices of money or time to support a position she holds. What might this tell her about her love of comfort? And how much should any of us love appearing proper or being comfortable anyway? Perhaps not all of us are being called to surrender all propriety or comfort, but that doesn't mean we shouldn't be wondering how much we should want to give over in their pursuit. Interrogating our fears reveals our loves. As our loves are revealed—as they're brought to consciousness—we can compare what we actually love to what we think is worth our love. And as we do so, we are better equipped to evaluate which among our fears is worth attending to and how much attention to give them: fearing persecution and fearing embarrassment are not worth giving equal weight. All Christians are called to *witness*, but not all of us are called to be witnesses (the Greek word is "martyr") in the same way.

At the risk of oversimplifying things, we might think of the relation between confession and witness in this way: Where Christians confess in order to orient ourselves in space and time, we witness in order to describe what we see God doing around us in that space and time, namely, pursuing love-shaped justice. Obviously, that distinction collapses: Christians orient themselves in light of God's work in and around them. Yet the distinction also holds: as we become aware of where we are before God in the world, we become aware of where God is acting in the world.

To witness is to give voice to that awareness. Because God's transformation of the world is underway, part of what love does in ordering our fears is help us to distinguish between the fears that come with giving up on the things that are passing away, the fears that come with facing those things that resist that transformation, and the fear (perhaps "awe" might be a better word here) of the God whose holy love drives that transformation.

As witnesses, we discover that Christian love *overcomes* our fears by situating them within a larger vision of God's loving actions in the world. In a vision of the world in which we are each discrete and relatively autonomous individuals, avoiding conversations as a way of avoiding arguments may seem like a pretty good idea. Better to go through the world untouched by others than to go through it roughed up by them. But in a Christian vision of the world, we are always already in relationship with others. Fearing conversation with them not only inhibits the possibility of developing those relationships, it actually ignores the degree to which those relationships are already shaping us.

It may be that we fear the possible tensions that such conversations would lead to. Many of us have experienced occasions of discomfort when asked by a friend or colleague to talk about faith. Such discomfort is frequently the consequence of feeling like that friend or colleague is responding to some sense of imposed obligation that leaves us wondering whether our relationship is actually valued for its own sake. Some of us have probably pursued such artificial conversations or artificial relationships. We are, understandably, fearful of such conversations.

Or perhaps we fear that our conversations will lead to arguments. In a society in which debates between Christians and atheists actually draw crowds and make money, it's hard not to wonder whether conversations about faith are inherently oppositional. Of course, it may also be that those conversations become occasions in which we are reminded of our own shortcomings—including a willingness to move too quickly into argument. This side of eternity, such results are not only possible but often seem likely.

Both the fear of using another and the fear of getting into an argument reveal our concern that talking about faith disrupts, rather than enhances, relationships. Experience and conventional wisdom affirm this fear. But allowing this fear to hold sway in our lives has the effect of displacing the very thing that makes those relationships—whether actual or potential—meaningful; namely, our open, honest, and vulnerable communication with others. After all, whatever else it means, loving our neighbors—our friends and colleagues and family—means talking with them and loving them as ourselves means being vulnerable enough to hear what they have to say, even if what they say isn't always welcome news to us.

Significantly, in talking with our neighbors and being vulnerable to their insights, we are reminded of our deepest longing: a longing for *communion*, for a life lived in transparent and joyful participation with others in God. That is, love overcomes our fears in a temporary and halting way because these loves mirror and are founded in God's perfect love in which there is no fear because it has been replaced by our being utterly present to each other in God.

The term "communion" may mislead some since it more frequently refers to the celebration of the Eucharist or the Lord's Supper in the church. The point of that celebration is to mark not simply an event in the past—Jesus' last supper with his disciples—but to participate in a partial and fuzzy way in the new community inaugurated by that meal and the events that immediately followed. So rather than distance my use of the term from that more frequent reference, I would suggest that the vision of union with God and others that we see in the Eucharist might be an orienting vision for how we might relate to all those around us in our daily lives—including those with whom we interact in the public square. Indeed, politics as it is infused with love becomes nothing less than the project of living into the promised communion with God and with others that comes in the Kingdom of God. Ultimately, both confession and witness point toward the reconciliation—within persons, between persons, and with God—that is synonymous with communion. We confess and we witness as ways of learning what it means to live in communion.

So: in opposing our fears, love shapes a life of confession—a life in which we recognize our place with others before God during this world. In ordering our fears, love shapes a life of witness—a life in which we share through our own words what we see God doing right now. And in overcoming our fears, love shapes a life of communion—a life in which we are being transformed into citizens of the Kingdom of God.

A brief tangent: At least stereotypically, Christians enter the public sphere as evangelists; seeking to save "lost souls" from the fires of hell, we go out seeking to convert people to Christianity. In the popular imagination, this usually involves awkward conversations with strangers who, though usually polite, seem intent on achieving a goal (often determined by numbers) and moving on. Respecting the courage and integrity of persons who pursue such projects, I hope nonetheless that this brief excursus into the relation of fear and love (and, therein, to confession, witness, and communion) clarifies the problems with such an approach. Assuming they "carry" Christ into their conversations, such evangelists mislocate themselves and therein miss the power of confession. Assuming God does not work apart from human will, such evangelists betray their own blindness to what God is already doing in the world—including in the lives of those they are attempting to convert—and therein miss the wisdom of witness. Assuming that hit-and-run evangelism is adequate to the task of conversion, they ignore the larger reconciling purposes of conversion and therein miss the uniting power of communion. In all this, they reveal the degree to which their fears drive their loves rather than letting love oppose, order, and overcome their fears. Ironically, then, this type of evangelism is not only inimical to the good news that stimulates confession, shares itself in witness, and longs for communion, it undermines the coherence of Christian love expressed in the public square.

This side of eternity, we will not love perfectly. Our confessions will be halting and used as expressions of self-righteousness; our witness will be misguided and shaped by our various projects of self-justification; and our communion incomplete and caught up in projects of exclusion. As we believe aloud, we will make public our mis-belief because as we act in love we will also reveal just how disordered our loves are. But our response to our mis-beliefs cannot intelligibly be the refusal to believe or to speak for it is through belief and conversation that we are being transformed by a loving God. Opposing, ordering, overcoming: love does this to our fears. Confessing, bearing witness, and longing for communion: love induces these things in us as it challenges our fears.

Love and Christian Vision

In cultivating discontentment, love prevents us from settling for the world as it is by helping us resist the urges to see the world as finished and ourselves as complete. That is, love calls us to fight against our urges to see things too clearly because they have not yet actually come into focus. In challenging fear, love prevents us from submitting to the world as it is by helping us resist the urge to see the world as malevolent and ourselves as its victims. That is, love calls us to fight against our urges to hide our eyes from the world because it isn't as foul as we make it out to be. Love, then, reveals the narrow path between trying to see too much and trying to see too little; between arrogantly claiming to know too much and fearfully refusing to learn more; between accepting our desires as we've currently shaped them and squelching our desires out of fear of what they will bring us. It trains us in both humility and courage.

How, though, does this play out in the process of learning to see as God sees and, therein, engage the public in loving ways? It does so, I think, through two processes that flow out of cultivated discontentment and challenged fear. Against contentment, love pushes us to expand our vision of what is going on in the world. And against fear, love encourages us to see the world in holistic ways. That is, expansion and holism are the political expressions of love's cultivation of discontentment and challenge to fear.

First, love motivates us to expand the range of things that we are willing to look at. All too often in public matters, we seize on a single idea or opinion and let it shape our expressions of public engagement. We reduce our vision to fit whatever ideologies, soundbytes, or bumper stickers happen to mesh with our prior prejudices or those of our heroes—as if either the government or the free market, either self-reliance or community, either technology or simplicity, either military might or pacifism were panaceas for our problems. We become nearsighted, unable or unwilling to look into the distance at a large, complex, interdependent, and changing world. We structure our public and political activities in light of our vision problem and think that others do the same. Most of the interesting problems in the world, though, cannot be reduced to slogans or isolated from other systems, so attempting to solve them—as if such solutions were even within our grasp—with simple tools in near blindness is far more likely to exacerbate those problems than address them.

But we can see more than our favored politicians, pundits, and prognosticators invite us to look at. Loved by God, we can begin to make connections between disparate events and peoples and then test those connections—something I tried to do in "The New Odd Couple?"* Love invites us to ask more questions, to look from more sides, to make wider connections, to recognize the limits of our own vision in the process, and to be surprised by the new things that we may see. It motivates us to spend the time and energy necessary in interpreting what God is doing in the world, how histories, cultures, and their interactions have shaped the actors in any set of events, how those actors are, themselves, interpreting those events, and how our own discernment of God at work in our individual lives is shaping the decisions we make and the actions we take. In shorthand, love pushes us to enlarge our vision and act in light of—rather than in denial of—that larger vision.

Toward that end, there are a range of practices we can take up: read better newspapers and journals—including those that feature columnists with whom we may disagree. Study history. Find places to meet and talk with people who are not like us. Occasionally pick up and read a substantive work of literature. Resist our tendencies to nod with or against the talking heads on the news. Go to the kind of church that asks us to think—but not all to think the same. Pray.

As our vision is enlarged—as we learn to see more from more sides— we will discover that the world and the people in it cannot be reduced to simple either/or's: either good or bad; either right or wrong; either friend or foe; either clean or dirty. Where fear encourages us to divide the world into two, love motivates us to look at the world in more holistic ways. All too often in public matters, we are grasped by fears that are disproportionate to threats and we construct divisions that reinforce those fears. We look at the world in black-and-white rather than color, living in gated communities, stockpiling weapons, dismantling playground toys, and all-but bathing in Purell. The world, though, is a far messier place than such dualisms admit and the problems that we face in it are neither black-and-white nor even shades of gray. They are prismatic and multihued, showing different color combinations as the light of human wisdom strikes them from many angles.

Loved by God, though, we can begin to break down our simple sets of opposites, seeing points of consonance, overlap, and complexity. Loved by God, we have the courage to see that we can't remove problems from our midst when we are culpable in making and exacerbating them and that we can actually address those problems better from their midst than from a distance—which was, I think, part of my point in following up "Soldiers and Saints" with "A Moral Equivalent to Penance."* Love finds connections: individual and systemic, innocence and guilt, near and far. It attends to the things we share without dismissing the things that make us distinct. It reveals the illusions upon which dualisms are based and connects the present to both a past too complex to be described in terms of simple causes and effects and to a future in which God is reconciling all things to Herself. Love doesn't mean not acting in public settings as a way of keeping oneself pure. It means admitting our impurities and therein beginning to act in more sophisticated and coherent ways.

Toward that end, there are still more practices we can take up: Volunteer for programs where we meet people different from us by serving at soup kitchens, tutoring in ESL programs, or driving the families of inmates to and from prisons. Try to state the opinions of those with whom we disagree in ways that they would recognize. Pay attention to the way systems shape individuals and to which systems are shaping us. Travel abroad and eat exotic foods in local restaurants. Read Scripture. Talk with someone who practices a different faith. Above all, find a place where the power and goodness of God are emphasized. Pray.

Taking up such practices as those named above, when done as *practice*, helps make us into the kinds of people who can take up other, more controversial and explicitly political practices (such as writing letters to the editor, campaigning for candidates, attending town hall meetings, running for office, joining watchdog groups, boycotting companies that mistreat workers, voting, etc.) in ways that are shaped by love.

I have thus far mostly avoided explicit citations from Scripture. As I conclude this chapter, though, the words from St. Paul's first letter to the church in Corinth echo in my thoughts as a fitting conclusion. Usually heard at weddings, perhaps these sentences from 1 Corinthians 13 can also speak to those of us trying to believe aloud:

> If I speak in the tongues of mortals and of angels, but do not have love, I am a noisy gong or a clanging cymbal. And if I have prophetic powers, and understand all mysteries and all knowledge, and if I have all faith, so as to remove mountains, but do not have love, I am nothing. If I give away all my possessions, and if I hand

over my body so that I may boast, but do not have love, I gain nothing.

Love is patient; love is kind; love is not envious or boastful or arrogant or rude. It does not insist on its own way; it is not irritable or resentful; it does not rejoice in wrongdoing, but rejoices in the truth. It bears all things, believes all things, hopes all things, endures all things.

Love never ends. But as for prophecies, they will come to an end; as for tongues, they will cease; as for knowledge, it will come to an end. For we know only in part, and we prophesy only in part; but when the complete comes, the partial will come to an end. When I was a child, I spoke like a child, I thought like a child, I reasoned like a child; when I became an adult, I put an end to childish ways. For now we see in a mirror, dimly, but then we will see face to face. Now I know only in part; then I will know fully, even as I have been fully known. And now faith, hope, and love abide, these three; and the greatest of these is love.

Tortured Logic

(Appeared October 21, 2007)

I have, of late, been asked repeatedly to sign various "Say No to Torture" statements. This makes me extremely depressed.

What do we know about torture? We know from expert after expert that it isn't effective in gaining useful information from the types of people most likely to have that information. We know that there are both national and international bans on the use of torture, many of those international bans initiated by the U.S. We know that, as Jean Améry puts it in his book, *At the Mind's Limits*, "torture is the most horrible event a human being can retain within himself." We know that recent polls from the Pew Research Center for the People and the Press show that roughly 45 percent of Americans think torture is often or sometimes justified against suspected terrorists. And in light of various revelations with regard to Presidential signing statements, extraordinary renditions, photos from Abu Ghraib prison, and the fact that the current administration (or at least significant members thereof) continues to support morally questionable interrogation techniques (including some that even the Pentagon has banned in its latest revisions to the U.S. Army Field Manual), we ought to be at least suspicious that its public denial of torture means it has twisted definitions to the point of breaking. In short, we know that torture is ineffective, illegal, immoral, but nonetheless popular and likely still being practiced in our names.

How can this be??? Why are we even having conversations about its permissibility?

Is it the popularity of "24" and movies in which the heroes make use of it? Maybe that's a symptom— perhaps it's even an exacerbating factor—but it's hard to believe that it's a cause. Only those on the far right and unthinking left continue to believe that the media's effect on culture can be understood via simple cause-effect relationships.

Is it because we've had the weakest Attorney General in recent history in charge of the Justice Department? No: Alberto Gonzalez may be foolish, forgetful, and unfortunately more faithful to his former boss than to the Constitution of the United States, but it's hard to place this at his doorstep.

Is it because the new age and the new war that dawned on 9/11 demand a new set of rules to replace those no longer able to address new terrors? While such may be the excuse, it isn't likely to be the cause: such dispensationalism here, like elsewhere, demands a vision of history so contorted that it will collapse in the face of historical analysis.

Is it because the current administration—like all administrations, whether Democratic or Republican—is interested in extending the scope of its power against the Judiciary or Congress? Or that Cheney, Rumsfeld, et al. are simply evil men? No. While the current administration may have had the opportunity to take advantage of and manipulate popular opinion, it isn't the case that they can simply manufacture that opinion. Our continued willingness to be led—even in morally abhorrent directions—turns on the possibility of our willingness to go that direction anyway.

Is it that we've long practiced torture and now have decided to be more honest about it? I hope not. Like Graham Green, I think I'd

prefer hypocrisy to honesty without conscience. At least such hypocrisy doesn't presume to make something morally abhorrent into something okay.

Is it just that most people are ignorant—perhaps intentionally so—of torture's failings? That many of us actually believe torture works because we've seen it work on television and imagine that it would work if it were tried on us? Or that since we don't have to see it practiced (apart from in a stylized media-friendly format), we don't actually think it's something we need to worry about? Perhaps. But distance and apathy won't fully account for our current fascination with torture and its "uses," nor for our willingness to permit it. After all, some issues (e.g., abortion, homosexuality), when dealt with in the abstract, have tended toward more restrictive, rather than more permissive, popular opinions.

There is one other thing we know about torture: that it turns out not to be about the acquisition of information but the expression of control—in this instance, the attempt to control, at visceral levels, the mind and body of another human being. So could it be that the reason U.S. society is even having conversations about torture is that after 9/11 (and perhaps even more acutely, in light of our discoveries about the limits of our power in Afghanistan and Iraq), we simply are not sure about how much control we do or ought to have in our own lives and in the world? That no matter the rational arguments for and against or the herd mentality of popular opinion, this is an issue currently driven by our ids, rather than our egos? That we're willing to contemplate torture in the abstract in order to preserve the fallacies of our invulnerability? Probably.

But if that's the case, then two conclusions follow. First, feeding our ids will only make matters worse: the effect of accepting the torture of another human being in order to maintain our own sense of control will inevitably lead us to question that very control if we live in a world where torture happens. And second, the project of re-establishing whatever solidity there may be to the position that all torture at all times should be prohibited isn't going to turn on what we know about torture, but what we feel about it. And toward that end, the conversations that our society is currently having about torture are going to have to be internal as well. Said differently, opposition to torture won't turn on education alone, but on conversion as well. And that—as religious thinkers have long pointed out—is a much more complicated project than just signing a "Say No to Torture" statement.

Childhood Fetish

(Appeared January 28, 2007)

The social critic Christopher Lasch has suggested that one of the best ways to get a sense of what a culture thinks about the future is to ask about how it treats its children. When Lasch wrote *The Culture of Narcissism* in the late 1970s, he opined that since children were either ignored or denigrated, Western culture had a fairly bleak opinion of its future. I wonder what he would say today.

If the advent of affordable and effective birth control and the legalization of abortion were conceptual focal points for social understandings of procreation in the '60s and '70s, *in vitro* fertilization and the advent of fertility clinics were foci of the '80s and '90s. Thus, where the children of the '70s were ignored, the so-called "Millennial Generation" (those born after 1981) is adored. We began protecting them with "Baby on Board" signs and continued to do so as "Soccer Moms" morphed into "Security Moms." We began taking unnecessary pictures of them *in utero* (glamour shots of fetuses???) and now buy them "My Twin" dolls. We comparison-shop for the best daycare programs and compare our toddlers to their class-mates to see who is furthest along developmentally: Can Johnny stack blocks? Does Susie understand two-step instructions? Millennial children have been desired, defended, driven, and doted upon.

Assuming Lasch is right (which, I admit, is a major though provocative assumption), does that mean that we think the future is bright and hope-filled? Have we become optimists about what will come? Do we believe ours is a future to value? Perhaps. But probably not. Given the proliferation of apocalyptic literature—whether of the religious, ecological, economical, viral, or nuclear persuasion—it's hard to accept that conclusion. And even setting aside all those parents raising millennial children as a means of reaffirming their own worth (Lasch's book was, after all, about narcissism), it's hard to imagine how being over-scheduled, over-protected, and over-indulged is an expression of being valued. If anything, it's a sign that we don't know how to value children. We've turned children into fetishes.

For those of you who associate the word "fetish" with various idiosyncratic libidinal energies (and are now trying to decide whether to associate me with various sexually abhorrent practices),

I should probably define the term. In economic circles, a fetish is a thing whose natural worth has been hidden by its socially determined value: a diamond is valued not because it is hard but because it is a symbol of love. In anthropological circles, a fetish is any object that is believed to have supernatural powers: a four-leafed clover brings good luck. In this editorial, I'm blurring the economic and anthropological meanings: knowing children are valuable but not sure why, we are easily seduced into casting spells to secure them against impending doom.

First, we lack a clear sense of why children are valuable and so we rely on socially determined claims about their value. But many of the older religious reasons for valuing children (e.g., they are gifts from God or signs of blessing) have become less interesting in a society that seldom attends to the transcendent and less culturally compelling in a society that accepts religious pluralism. And many of the older irreligious reasons for valuing children (e.g., as a means of labor in agrarian cultures or as a sort of social security in old age) have faded in importance.

They've been replaced by absurd non-sequiturs ("I believe the children are our future") and not-so-absurd-but-not-existentially-compelling claims about the universal rights of children as fellow human beings. And when those claims aren't adequate to describe the actual feelings we have for our own children, we practice a bit of linguistic sleight-of-hand: children aren't valuable; they're *invaluable.*

Then, having surrendered the work of thinking about what makes children valuable, we're left to attempt the impossible. Since they're invaluable, they must be exhaustively protected. And so we attempt to secure their future for them through the thoroughly enchanted notion that being preoccupied with them now will ward off contingency in the future. The problem, of course, is that none of us can know or control the future. The future-fearing project of fetishizing our children is, itself, doomed.

At one level, parents know this project is absurd. No matter our efforts, children never turn out just like we hope or achieve just what we think they should. But the social pressure to deny that knowledge, compounded as it is by the practical fear that we put our own children at a disadvantage when they compete against the children of parents who ignore the project's absurdity, leaves us vulnerable to the absurd.

Even worse, it leaves our children without a functional sense of their own worth or a hopeful vision for their own future. Which is unfortunate in every sense of that word, as those are among the most important things one generation can pass to another.

A New Fundamentalism, Part I

(Appeared May 13, 2007)

In his book *Among the Believers: An Islamic Journey*, Nobel prize-winner V. S. Naipaul gives one of the most trenchant descriptions of fundamentalism I know. Writing on the failures of Pakistan to become the Muslim state its founders had desired, he observes, "The state withered. But faith didn't. Failure only led back to the faith. The state had been founded as a homeland for Muslims. If the state failed, it wasn't because the dream was flawed, or the faith flawed; it could only be because men had failed the faith. A purer and purer faith began to be called for. . . [and] men lost sight of the political origins of their state." There are other far more empirically detailed and intellectually developed definitions of the political expression of fundamentalism, but for my money, I'll take Naipaul's. A political fundamentalist is someone who, when a political system fails to achieve all that was hoped, blames that failure on the impurity of its leaders and calls for a new generation of purer leaders.

I thought about Naipaul's description when reading of the Washington scandals of the past few weeks—members of the Bush administration caught up in possible prostitution rings; George Tenet arguing that that same administration took his "slam dunk" comment out of context (how much context can "slam dunk" take, by the way?) and laying blame for failures in Iraq on other parties; falsehoods about Jessica Lynch and Pat Tillman. Given the long history of political scandals, why are we shocked by these latest? Other than insisting that we're scandalized as a means of maintaining the illusions of our own innocence, I imagine that these scandals feel particularly acute because the guilty parties surfed into power on waves of indignation about the moral failings of their predecessors. Remember: in 2000, George W. Bush ran on a platform of bringing honor and decorum back to the Clinton-besmirched White House, challenging an interventionist foreign policy that was commingled with lack of attention to military welfare, and rejecting slick bait-and-switch political chicanery.

I'm not interested in promoting a nostalgic look back at the Clinton White House as a time when things weren't that bad (nostalgia for what never actually was being another oft-appearing characteristic of fundamentalism) nor of revel-

ing in the peculiar *schadenfreude* of politicians hoisted upon their own petards (ironic detachment being one of the liberal vices that energizes fundamentalist reactivism). I am, however, wondering just how damaging to our political processes it must be when purity is extolled as a political virtue and campaigns are reduced to "we'd never do that!" sloganeering. So I have a hypothesis that I want to test over the next few weeks. It is that we are witnessing (participating in, really) a new and peculiar kind of democratic fundamentalism that is increasingly driving American politics.

The depth of such fundamentalism is revealed in the fact that the bow toward purity isn't confined to one political party but seems to pervade them all. Republicans and Democrats rely on it—as do most citizens, given the degree to which we view the recent scandals principally as scandals rather than errors, outrages, or idiocies. We're all fundamentalists and will remain so as long as we continue to extol purity as a fundamental political virtue. If you doubt this applies to you, ask yourself: "Have I ever voted for a candidate because I'd be less embarrassed with him in office than I am with the current office holder?" "Have I ever favored a candidate because I thought she was more virtuous than her opponents?" "Do I think that the right person in charge will resolve the problems I see right now?" If you answer any of those questions affirmatively, you might be a political fundamentalist.

The preoccupation with purity that marks this new kind of political fundamentalism leaves artifice ascendant even as growing suspicion and ignorance by citizens of how government works helps found it. Increased media attention to the "horse race" among competing campaigns or candidate charisma and religious background feeds it. A preoccupation with hypocrisy as worst among political vices reinforces it. And thinking that the right person can fix politics solidifies it.

None of this is to say that integrity, trustworthiness, charisma, or other individual virtues should be ignored. They are important components of good leadership. It is, instead, to say that they ought not be paramount in electing our leaders. Political fundamentalism, like all fundamentalisms, suffers from an inability to recognize and thereby begin to address its own flaws. And given the complexity of the world, such an inability leaves its adherents with a kind of ideological whiplash as they are yanked

between unfounded optimism and unconsidered pessimism.

Because the world behaves in irreducibly complex ways, states— especially in constitutional democracies like our own—address that complexity by developing sophisticated systems of statecraft, and since resolving one political dilemma will usually create new ones, no politician—no matter how marvelous he or she might be—can fix everything for us. This isn't to say we ought to give up. But we ought to be a bit more chastened in our enthusiasms and cautious in ennui.

Soldiers and Saints
(Appeared December 3, 2006)

To judge from the prevailing political winds, we should see more and more soldiers returning home from Iraq over the next several months. Prominent Democrats are nearsightedly calling for withdrawal from that country (like that will help to stabilize a country now more at war with itself than U.S. forces). Prominent Republicans are meanspiritedly damning the Iraqis for not taking responsibility for their country (conveniently forgetting the Powell-Pottery Barn doctrine of "you break it, you bought it"). And the majority of the U.S. population is scrupulously revising its history so that they aren't part of the majority that once thought invading Iraq was a good idea.

I don't envy those returning soldiers.

Like the ones that returned from Vietnam, they face some tough times ahead. Unlike Vietnam vets, though, those times aren't likely to involve things like getting called "baby-killer" and being spat upon. Instead, they're going to be expected to live up to standards that nobody can attain.

At least to judge from the various emails I receive, talk-radio hosts I hear, editorials I read, and "Support Our Troops" bumper stickers I see, today's soldiers in Iraq have John Wayne's guts, Mother Theresa's compassion, Nathan Hale's patriotism, Solomon's wisdom, and Tiger Woods' discipline. Saying anything that can even be perceived as mean toward soldiers can get one socially blackballed—just ask John Kerry. Even noted Bush-opponent and "Doonesbury" writer Garry Trudeau makes Iraqi soldiers into heroes. Iraqi vets are so respected that they can actually get elected to Congress—as Democrats, no less.

I'm not saying that the vast majority of today's armed forces aren't doing something noble and difficult. Nor am I saying that they don't deserve recognition for the sacrifices they make. Nor, even, am I saying that some of our men and women in the military haven't done mind-bogglingly heroic and sacrificial things. As a whole, they have taken on a difficult task for which they deserve our appreciation; individually, some have done things that deserve our awe.

But what happens when they return and we discover that they are just as likely to speed through school zones, curse at co-workers, and write absurd letters-to-the-editor as the rest of us? What happens when they return and we discover that they are struggling with some of the deeply disturbing things they saw and did? As our society grows ever less forgiving and ever more likely to confuse vengeance with justice, what happens when they do things or say things that may need forgiveness or justice? If we haven't been willing to shell out the tax-dollars and compassion necessary to fully fund yesterday's veterans, are we really likely to do it when tomorrow's veterans turn out not to be the paragons of virtue we've imagined them to be? Beatifying them now will only give us an excuse to condemn them later.

Please don't misunderstand me: I am not opposed to military service in principle—though like missionaries, I think that the ultimate goal of those in the military is to work themselves out of a job. I have good friends that either are or have served in the military and had I not entered seminary, I was *this close* to joining the Air Force as a way of putting myself through medical school. When asked why they enlisted, these friends say some combination of the following: To serve my country. To make a better life for myself. I wasn't sure what else to do. To learn to kill people and blow stuff up. And here's the thing:

none of them give just that first reason and most admit to the last one. To a person, they're human, and military service no more made them superhuman than the absence of military service prevented others from doing extraordinary things.

Think soldiers are the only ones that make sacrifices for their country? Tell that to the wife of a former marine and friend of mine who has repeatedly turned down plush suburban teaching jobs in order to teach in inner-city schools because she sees their need and thinks there is almost nothing more important in democratic societies than an educated populace. Think soldiers are the only ones who have made our country free? Tell that to my friend the retired public official and former Army lieutenant who says some of his toughest battles were fought defending the right of people to say things that most people disagreed with. Think soldiers are the only ones willing to endure hardship in order to help those in desperate need living under despotic regimes? Tell that to the daughter of another friend who is giving years of her life to serve in the Peace Corps in Sudan.

Today's soldiers deserve our support not because they are saints but because they are human and, as human beings, they will do things both profound and petty, both honorable and horrible, both gallant and ghastly. If we cannot learn to support them because they are human and, as human, worthy of our care, we only reveal the petty, horrible, and ghastly in ourselves. And if we can learn to support them because they are human, perhaps we can learn something about caring for all those other humans around us that we're so quick to ignore, damn, or beatify.

The Indignant and the Indigent
(March 11, 2007)

Defending the indigent has never been politically popular. Most of us—myself included—would prefer to approach indigent defense the same way we tend to approach the indigent: only briefly, only if we don't have to make eye contact, and only if we can't find an alternative route. So it's no surprise that the state of Georgia took more than forty years to establish a statewide public defender system. Legislators would rather not wrestle with it, rather not be forced to look at it from within a Constitutional framework, and rather not allow it near the top of their lists of things to do.

Nonetheless, through the consistent and hard work of lawyers, reporters, and other concerned citizens, the state was able to replace a wide range of local approaches—many of which were not so much inadequate as utterly incompetent—with a statewide system that brought needed attention, clarity, and support to the system, and now operates under the Georgia Public Defenders Council. And while most of those who helped shape the system are the first to admit that it has its weaknesses, they'll also tell you it was a huge step forward.

Now legislators want to take steps backward.

Bills currently before the state legislature are attempting to allow circuit courts to drop out of the system, move the Georgia Public Standards Council from the judicial to the executive branch, change the composition of the Council, and give permission to the General Assembly not to provide for that council's annual budget, among other things.

The named reason behind all these bills is to establish greater oversight on the Council and tighter accountability over the Council's budget. It's debatable whether that's the actual reason though: the Council is already under a legislative oversight committee and already provides budget documents to that committee. And expenses come from fees and fines administered by the court system rather than taxes. So why else might these bills be coming before the state legislature? For one thing, the legislature has moved to the right since the state system was established. And for another, it's hard for state lawmakers to work up much energy toward defending a system that defends people who (a) have been accused

of crimes, and (b) most of us don't want to deal with anyway.

As happens with most bills, this batch would almost certainly have undergone revision as they went through the legislature. Sometimes that process makes for better law. Usually it makes for laws that more closely reflect the political will of the current legislature. And most times that's all to the good: the process beats its alternatives and in most cases it's important that a current legislature not be permitted to tie the hands of future ones.

This time, though, it won't be good because this time indigent defense has a face: Brian Nichols. As the process of moving Nichols to and through trial becomes more and more costly, the desires both to control the costs of indigent defense and also to separate ourselves from the indigent (or, more accurately, to separate the indigent from us) grow ever stronger. As a result, the political will on the part of our elected officials to defend the state system which was never strong to begin with is likely to grow even weaker.

Being indignant at what Nichols did is perfectly reasonable—as is being indignant at the costs associated with his trial. Indeed, our degree of indignation is part of the reason the Nichols trial is so expensive since it contributes to the D.A.'s insistence on the more costly process of seeking the death penalty—though overcharging by the D.A. hasn't helped. But letting our indignation at the Nichols trial shape the future of indigent defense is a bad idea.

No matter our personal attitudes toward Nichols in particular or the indigent in general, their right to adequate counsel and a fair trial is a constitutional mandate and a sign of our society's health. Maintaining a fair and independent statewide system of indigent defense is our society's way of saying that we are confident enough in our stability and fortitude to accept the existence of those members of society we'd rather not see. It's also one way of being clear-sighted enough to recognize that sometimes the indigent are in the place they are because society already let them down and that whether we want to deal with them or not, the indigent are part of our society.

Among the members of the church my wife serves is a man named Charlie. He's had a rough life—quite a bit of which, by his own admission, he brought on himself. He spends more nights on the streets than he ought and struggles daily to make his way in the world, but it's a struggle he keeps at. He's also the first one to applaud the choir after an anthem, no matter how they sound. It's a generous act of appreciation that the church is learning from. When you look at Georgia's indigent defense system, try to see Charlie. And if you won't see indigent defense as a matter of justice for him, maybe you can at least emulate his generosity.

Making Ourselves at Home
(Appeared January 6, 2008)

*Genuine homesickness was not
self-pity, but rather self-destruction.
It consisted in dismantling our past
piece by piece, which could not be
done without self-contempt and
hatred for the lost self.*
—Jean Améry

Over the past few weeks, I've been
exploring the way the current presidential candidates tell the story of
American history—partly because
it's good to know how they understand the traditions they stand in
before voting, but more importantly
because they're the first set of presidential candidates that must include
9/11 and what followed from it in
the way they tell that history. The
trick is that 9/11 and following created such dramatic upheaval in the
U.S. that they have had the effect of
actually changing the way many of
us understand U.S. history before
2001. And since the new narrative
of our long history isn't settled, the
candidates are currently telling different stories. From John Edwards'
"Two Americas" to Tom Tancredo's
"One Highly Guarded America";
from Ron Paul's libertarian world to
Hillary Clinton's "First Lady Woman
in the White House": American his-

tory is, itself, being contested right
now.

This is no surprise. Contested
storytelling always follows upheaval. Indeed, one way to read U.S.
history is as a series of re-told narratives, each building on but distinct
from the previous: the narrative of
exploration and new space replaced
by one of revolution and political
liberty replaced by one of equality
and national unity replaced by one
of growth and international power,
etc. Since things change and no
narrative is perfect, our national
narrative is always dynamic. Some
disruptions are bigger than others,
however, and 9/11 was big, if only
because it disrupted a national narrative of homeland invulnerability
and economic security. So what will
American history look like now?

One bad way to tell history is
to confuse it with nostalgia, making
the past look sunnier either to appeal to voters' own nostalgic sense of
times gone by or to make the present look more dangerous. Another
bad way to tell history is to treat the
tools of the past as unhelpful to deal
with today's concerns and thereby
to treat the past with antipathy. The
former leads to beatifying past leaders (note the spate of biographies
released over the past six years),
wooden interpretations of the

Constitution, and huge ineffective walls along our southern border. The latter leads to grandiose claims about the powers of the presidency, an ignored Bill of Rights, and a willingness to contemplate torture. It is hard to imagine Americans—past or present—who, upon reflection, would say, "Yes, that is what I want America to be like."

But what would they say? Part of the trick in telling American history is dealing with Americans' forward-thinking sensibility. More than many countries (one thinks of those of Europe, for example), America has been future-oriented and, therefore, has been deliberate about telling its history in a way that is open ended. The starting question hasn't been, "How did we get to this point in time?" It's been "Who do we want to be in the future?" We've thought of history more as preface than plotline.

That question has become far more complex as the U.S. increasingly recognizes its interdependence with the rest of the world (9/11 being, among other things, a sign of that interdependence) and as we've moved from production-based to consumption-based capitalism (and therefore less future-oriented). There is simply less clarity about "we" and less attention to "to be."

If we can get past the temptations of nostalgia and antipathy toward the past (both being forms of homesickness as Jean Améry would describe it), we will still need to imagine a new narrative big enough to encompass interdependence, strong enough to deal with vulnerability, and wise enough to remain future-oriented. That will mean, moreover, that a compelling telling of U.S. history will explain how all those things—interdependence, vulnerability, and future-orientation—have always been a part of our national history.

I do not know what such a narrative will sound like (though I would not be surprised if it emphasizes those parts of our history that focus on oppressed groups who have overcome adversity by working together). My suspicion is that the youngest and the oldest of the current candidates, Barack Obama and John McCain, may be the most likely to be able to tell such a story if they would simply try to do so. If we can neither shape nor accept such a narrative, however, we will end up homesick—and then end up homeless.

Hocus Pocus

(Was not printed)

Apparently, our mothers were wrong. It's not just that sticks and stones may break our bones, but that words can ruin our lives. Joe Biden (always a stream-of-consciousness, non-stop talker) refers to Barack Obama as an "articulate and bright and clean and a nice-looking guy" and his presidential campaign is over. Ann Coulter (aka "Twiggy with Tourette's") calls John Edwards a "faggot" and liberal villagers scurry for torches and pitchforks. Don Imus (the original shock-jock, for Pete's sake!) describes the Rutgers women's basketball team as "nappy-headed ho's" and loses his job. Newt Gingrich (who doesn't even need a parenthetical note) implies Spanish is the language of the ghetto and is forced into a quick and even more embarrassing retraction/apology/explanation.

Let's be clear: every action described above was offensive, each speaker warranted being disciplined, and nobody should get to say whatever they want whenever they want. Words are potent and language-use has implications. But their potency is complex and those implications can't be measured by simple cause-effect models—facts which the current debates seem to ignore in our fixation on the words themselves. It's as if we've started to believe that words were magical.

At the high point of medieval mass in Roman Catholic churches, the priest would take a wafer, turn to face the crucifix, and recite the words of institution in Latin: *hoc est corpus meum:* "this is my body." Supposedly, since those in attendance could neither hear the priest clearly—what with his back turned to them—nor generally spoke Latin, those words over time became "hocus pocus": the magic words that turned bread into Jesus' body. We live in a differently enchanted world than did medieval Catholics and so don't risk eternal wrath for using magical words improperly. But we do face the historical wrath of the word-police for using certain words.

Again: let's be clear. There are a few words whose use is almost always offensive and there are any number of words that, used wrongly, are likely to offend. And some words, when used repeatedly and in the context of inequities of power, can cause long-lasting harm—though I doubt any of the examples above fit that context. But the attempt to create an offense-free society by banishing certain words, like any puritanical attempt to banish obscene language, is both doomed and wrong-headed. It's doomed because folks like Imus often want to offend in order to make a point and folks like Coulter want to offend because they're arrested in moral adolescence. Clucking at them to stop is like trying to end a battle by supplying the enemy with ammunition.

It's wrong-headed because it confuses offense with harm. None of the victims of the offensive language described above actually had their interests damaged as a result of that language and some actually benefited from the associated scandal. Joe Biden, for instance, gave Barack Obama a gift with his gaffe: Obama gained popular support for being the victim of Biden's ill-chosen words even as those same words remind voters of just how articulate, bright, and good looking he is as an individual regardless of his race.

Moreover, the real danger with confusing offense with harm is that it reinforces the very understanding of persons-as-victims that those troubled by offensive language ought to want to undermine. That is, it assumes that all other things being equal, people are so fragile that they can be damaged by offensive words.

This vision of human-as-fragile suggests we don't have the resources (e.g., a sense of self, resilience, fortitude, the ability to grow through adversity, etc.) that we actually need to cope with a world in which words hurt. And in the process, it imagines that the only way to discipline those who use offensive language is to punish them because they, like their victims, cannot grow, learn, or otherwise change.

Let me be clear one more time: words can hurt and we ought to be sympathetic to and interested in helping those who are victims of occasional hurtful language. And if we are interested in shaping a civil society, we ought to both refrain from offensive language and seek appropriate discipline for those who don't refrain. But we do the victims of offensive speech no favors by asking them to view themselves as harmed by that language; instead, we repeat the transgressions of the offenders by treating the victims as less than they are.

Because in the end, those who would abolish offensive speech by punishing offensive speakers get it almost exactly backwards: they treat words as magically powerful and people as fragile when it's actually the case that words, for all their potency, are remarkably ephemeral

and fragile things but people can be
pretty damn tough.

The (Ad)vantage of Democracy

(Appeared October 28, 2007)

Unbelievably, the primary campaign
season is likely to be all-but-over in
a little over three months. By the
end of January, so many state primaries will be completed that we'll
know which two candidates we'll
see on the ballots in November of
'08. So I'm sending out a call to all
ingenious inventor-types: if it's not
already too late, I'd like a campaign-
ad spam blocker for my television.

I'm tired of claims about how
various candidates can cure all that
ails us. And I'm not just talking
about the deliberately deceptive ads,
the fear-stoking ads, and the "my
opponent is an evil and moronic
butt-kisser who smells vaguely like
overcooked broccoli" ads. I'm talking about all of them—even the ones
that show happy pictures from family albums. In my worse moments I
could even be tempted to vote for a
candidate whose political platform
is, "Only yard signs and televised
debates allowed."

My problem with campaign
ads is that they work. In an age
when candidates' platforms are
boiled down to 15-second sound
bytes, I'd prefer to think that my
fellow-participants in this great

American democratic experiment are resistant to their charms, but that just isn't the case. Election after election, the ads succeed. And in succeeding, I wonder if they don't reveal a truth that is deeply unsettling—something that political advisors attend to but that the rest of us would rather not think about. For as I observe their effectiveness and their impact on the people with whom I talk politics, I've started to wonder whether the biggest political divide in the United States isn't red vs. blue, conservative vs. liberal, coastal vs. heartland, or rural vs. urban. It's cynic vs. utilitarian.

On the one side are the cynics—those who are so tired of feeling deceived, disappointed, or dictated to that they're tempted to quit on this whole "government of, by, and for the people" project. When they vote, they do so out of obligation but with a sense of resignation that most other voters (it's always "other voters") are voting for foolish reasons. And on the other side are the utilitarians, whose allegiances to political party, ideological vision, or personal advantage lead them to accept campaign ads as the foul means that serve their greater ends. When they vote, they do so out of a fear that things will go to hell if

other voters (it's still always "other voters") outnumber their side.

Is this what we've been reduced to? Are cynics and utilitarians replacing all those mythical responsible citizens of yesteryear? Have elections become political pageants full of platitudinous promises made by painstakingly polished candidates mouthing only the words we want them to say ("I'll keep us safe"; "I'll make us strong"; "A chicken in every pot and a Lexus in every garage") and leaving us wondering whether they could recognize an original thought should it rattle around in one of their well-coiffed heads? Are elections—the very things that most clearly define democracies—now destroying them?

In the dark moments of such thoughts, it helps to remember that one of the more profound defenses of democracy isn't that it is a wonderful form of government but that compared to other forms of government, it manages not to be a really bad one. Stable democracies regularly get things wrong, but they rarely get things horribly and tragically wrong. There are simply too many voices to hear and too many processes to get through for them to wander too far down the wrong road before someone starts advocating for another way or too quickly down that road before something makes us slow down. Democracies work because they recognize that people are likely to pursue their worse inclinations in the political sphere and so, rather than asking us to ignore those inclinations, they pit them against each other.

The Founding Fathers understood this. They knew that people would behave in self-contradictory ways (like cynics) and self-interested ways (like utilitarians). In fact, the Founding Fathers imagined that there was a bit of cynic and a bit of utilitarian in each of us—which isn't necessarily a bad thing. The inner cynic reminds us that no matter how passionate we may feel about a politician or position, we shouldn't accept their claims at face-value. The inner utilitarian reminds us that political issues matter even though they may not matter in the way politicians tell us. Cynics keep us from revolting; utilitarians keep us from surrendering.

So I'll put up with campaign ads. Even as they feed both the cynic and the utilitarian in me, they remind me that voting isn't meant to be a virtuous act so much as one that inhibits vices—including those of unconstrained cynicism and utilitarianism.

A Government of the People

(Appeared April 15, 2007)

Remembering Reagan is all the rage of late. Time Magazine featured a tearful version of him on the cover last month, my fellow columnist Eric Von Haessler wrote fondly of him last week, and historian John Patrick Diggins has an important if somewhat controversial new biography out on him arguing that Reagan typified the Emersonian tradition in American politics (which was news to some of my socialist-leaning Emersonian friends—but that's a conversation for another day).

In the spirit of the times, I'll contribute my own little piece to Reagomania by sharing a favorite Reagan quote (after all, whatever else anyone thinks of him, he was certainly quotable): "Government is like a baby: an alimentary canal with a big appetite at one end and no sense of responsibility at the other." I think about that quote this time of year while sending my check to the IRS.

Obviously, Reagan overstates. The government does have some sense of responsibility. Just ask the GAO or the many regulatory agencies that exist (regulation being the bureaucratic expression of responsibility, thereby making contemporary conservative calls for less regulation and more responsibility rather paradoxical). But Reagan did have a point: a government as big as ours takes a lot of money to run and is awfully hard to control even when—or perhaps especially when—politics aren't so partisan. At some point, even economies of scale fail.

Knowing where my money is going doesn't help. Take defense spending: the U.S. spends more on defense than the next twenty highest spenders combined. We still need to figure out how to pay for all the special appropriations that are helping fund the war in Iraq. And yet many members of Congress are afraid to even have a debate about cutting funding? Let's try this: let's peg defense spending to be equivalent to the amount paid by the next ten highest spending countries combined, take the remainder of our defense spending and . . . oh, I don't know: Fully fund health care for everyone under age eighteen? Service the national debt? End hunger? Build a wall across our northern border to keep out pesky Canucks? Give us all tax refunds? The options are endless. And don't get me started on how the government funds health care.

Oliver Wendell Holmes claimed that taxes are the price we pay for civilization. So as we pay our taxes, it's worth wondering: Are we behaving in civil ways? Are we showing regard for others? Are we caring for our neighbors? Are we speaking respectfully with and of others? Are we creating programs that benefit the least well off among us? Are we trying to shape a better future for the children? For that matter, are we trying to shape better children for the future? If taxes are the price we pay for civilization, I'm not sure we're getting our money's worth.

Maybe part of the problem is that we're not so different from Reagan's government baby: a big appetite for government goods at one end and no sense of responsibility at the other. After all, most of us are pretty happy to enjoy the benefits that come with living in a stable constitutional democracy, but for many of us that doesn't translate into going to the polling places (or voting based on a vision of the public good rather than our pocketbooks), volunteering in charitable organizations, writing our representatives, staying informed about matters of local and national interest, or trying to pay anything more than the least possible amount we can to the

IRS. Maybe it's not that we get the government we pay for so much as we are the government we pay for.

As a little test, try this as you make your way to the post office to send in your taxes: count the number of ways that the work of the state and federal government intersects with your journey. What systems of safety, infrastructure, subsidy, and service make your little trip easier? And each time you find a point of intersection, ask yourself whether you'd just-as-soon do without it (or, more accurately, have your citizens do without it). Even on a begrudged trip like this, perhaps we might find a bit of space for gratitude and a sense of responsibility that follows from that gratitude?

This time of year, there is much talk about better ways to set up the tax system. Simplify the current system. Move to a flat tax. Change to a fair tax. Certainly, the tax system can be improved upon. But setting up a new tax system without first asking what the present one reveals about us—and what our opinions about the present one reveal about the way we'll treat any tax system—isn't any more likely to help than remembering Reagan is likely to return us to the 1980s.

The New Odd Couple?

(February 11, 2007)

Environmentalists and evangelicals are, apparently, the new odd couple. Setting aside whatever debates they may have about the origins of the universe and human beings, the benefits of stem-cell research, and the obligation to teach about contraception, the two groups have come together to express a common concern about the dangers of global warming for the planet and its species. Thus, Harvard biologist E. O. Wilson writes an open letter to evangelicals, urging them to attend to the cries of creation and National Association of Evangelicals Vice President Richard Cizik encourages distributing bumper stickers that read "What Would Jesus Drive?" The press, especially, has been captivated by the two groups' common efforts—most recently, a collaborative effort by the Center for Health and the Global Environment at Harvard Medical School and the National Association of Evangelicals to produce "An Urgent Call to Action" about the dangers of fossil fuel consumption and species extinction.

Why shouldn't the press be captivated? The environmental movement is, obviously, composed of a bunch of left-wing, tree-hugging, corporate conspiracy-suspecting, Edward Abbey-reading Chicken Littles whose religious sensibilities tend toward either rationalist atheism or flights of druidic pantheism. And evangelicals are, just as obviously, a bunch of right-wing, Bible-thumping, rapture-believing, *Left Behind*-reading crusaders whose social sensibilities tend toward either Manichean escapism or Falwellian fulminations at godless culture.

Except they aren't. That we would think of evangelicals and environmentalists as an odd couple reveals more about our impoverished understandings of evangelicalism and environmentalism than it does about the way members of the two groups relate.

Begin with the question of who counts as an evangelical. A recent Baylor University study on American religious sensibilities discovered that more Christians in Mainline Protestant denominations identify themselves principally as "Evangelical" than those in Evangelical Protestant ones. That's a little like finding out that a greater percentage of African Americans like country music than Caucasians: after Charlie Pride, we knew such a thing could be the case, but our mental image of a country-music

aficionado (or evangelical) doesn't easily admit to such a thing. That same study found that the majority of Christians across theological and socio-historical lines favor greater involvement by the federal government in establishing a more even distribution of wealth, tighter regulations on business, and, especially, stronger protection of the environment, with over three fourths of Christians in all categories favoring better environmental protection. It would be hard to attribute that to environmentalist and seminary drop-out Al Gore!

And environmentalists? They're even harder to identify, given that environmentalism isn't so much a movement as a set of concerns about human impact on the natural world. As a biology major at Colorado College, a secular liberal arts college in the center of strongly evangelical Colorado Springs, I was constantly taking classes with and from a wide range of persons with a variety of religious, political, and scientific persuasions—but in the natural sciences, they were environmentalists to a person. One of my chemistry professors sang in an evangelical church choir and my (self-avowed evangelical) minister led backpacking trips on which we were as likely to read Henry David Thoreau as St. Paul's letter to the Romans. Whether you worshipped Gaia or Jehovah, you were encouraged to live by the three R's: Reduce. Reuse. Recycle.

Indeed, the surprise isn't that environmentalists and evangelicals might find common ground. It's that we haven't noticed how much common ground they've long shared. Evangelicalism and environmentalism are global movements of activists concerned about the salvation of the world through both social action and individual conversion. They also share that peculiar mix of cynicism about current social practices and optimism about transforming those practices through faith, reason, and hard work that is found in all idealists.

The question both groups must take up is whether idealism is adequate to the task of addressing the problems of global warming, environmental degradation, and species extinction. After all, whether any of us would use either label to describe ourselves, the vast majority of us think recycling is generally a good idea—though we're still likely to throw that empty soda can into the trash. Most of us think fuel efficiency is a good idea—though it seldom rises to the top of the list of priorities we use in buying a car.

Most of us like buying locally at farmers' markets—though we still usually shop at the supermarket. Our problem isn't that we disagree with the goals of environmental health; it's that our actions don't necessarily lead toward achieving them. So if environmentalists and evangelicals really want to do something together, they might think less about convincing us about what we ought to do and more about motivating us to do it.

And in the meantime, it may help us to be reminded that many of each group's concerns are not that different from the other's—nor are they that different from the rest of ours.

A Moral Equivalent of Penance

(Appeared September 16, 2007)

During the middle ages, soldiers returning from battle were required to do penance for anything they had done in battle that was motivated by hatred, pride, or passion. And they did this regardless of whether they believed that they were fighting for a just cause or not. The point of the penance was not only to address their misbehaviors in war, but to maintain clarity that behaviors deemed acceptable in battle are still unacceptable outside of it—and that since soldiers' lives are always bigger than the battles they fight, they would need some way to come to terms with their actions in battle so that they could re-enter society afterwards.

I was thinking about that as reports continue to come out about difficulties faced by soldiers returning from Iraq. Suicide rates up. Spousal abuse up. Divorce rates up. A growing demand for counseling by both military and civilian professionals and a growing awareness—at least by some—that seeking such counseling ought not be thought of as cowardly, wimpish, or unprofessional.

Adjusting to significant life-changes is never easy; it is far more difficult after returning from war. It always has been. My grandmother raised my mother and aunt on her own not because she didn't have a husband, but because the one she did have was mired in patterns of alcohol abuse, parental neglect, infidelity, and job delinquency. My grandfather simply couldn't return all the way from his time in the Asian theater of World War II. And at least according to conventional wisdom, the social struggles that veterans of the war in Vietnam faced were significantly shaped by popular antipathy to the roles they played there, thereby exacerbating their internal struggles. They received damnation rather than opportunities for penitence.

By contrast, the way most people talk about soldiers returning from Iraq, they have no need to do penance. Indeed, when even the military is having trouble prosecuting soldiers for clear violations of codes of conduct (as in Haditha), how could a civilian population that is convinced U.S. soldiers are in Iraq fighting for our freedom and is motivated by rolling waves of patriotic romanticism possibly gain the critical footing to help them distinguish good actions from bad in such complex circumstances? Left unsaid and too often unthought is the recognition that even if what soldiers are doing is for good, noble, and heroic reasons, it is nevertheless the case that many of the actions even the best among them take while at war are, nevertheless, unacceptable in any other context. Most soldiers I know are explicitly aware of this; the others seem at least to sense it.

To be clear: most of the soldiers I know acknowledge that they have behaved in ways that trouble them, but they did so because they believe that their actions help achieve values that are sufficiently important to warrant such behavior. Nonetheless, they are still troubled by their behavior. Removing the claim that these ways should be troubling has the effect of subverting their own principled sensibilities. It leaves them questioning the actual worth of the values they were affirming while doing the morally strange work of soldiers. Moreover, any national failure to recognize that such work is morally strange can only undermine our own claims to integrity and virtue when we defend our foreign policies. It simply is not in the national interest to look the other way.

The example from the middle ages got me to thinking. Setting

aside the fact that we are not a Roman Catholic country (not to mention the fact that as a Protestant, my understanding of repentance doesn't exactly square with Catholic notions of penance), shouldn't we be looking for a moral equivalent to penance? Not just therapy to help returning soldiers face their psychological struggles, but actual concrete opportunities for them to work through the social struggles they face as they re-enter society?

I don't know what this would look like, though my suspicion is that it might not be a bad idea to engage them in those types of tasks—doing relief work, building homes for the displaced, caring for "orphans and widows"—that are necessary for the constant rebuilding of society. Just as soldiers must engage in acts of destruction while in war, they can engage in acts of construction afterwards—not as a means of absolution, but as a way of re-learning and modeling how to live in the type of society that would be worth defending anyway. I know many do this anyway, but perhaps a country willing to put its military money where its political mouth is should think about ways that make such actions less a condition of individual will and more a declaration of national intent. It's just a thought.

5 Practicing and Practices

About ten months into writing weekly editorials, I received an email from a frustrated reader. His argument was that the four of us writing editorials weren't balanced: the two of us on the "left" are actually centrists and write on education and spirituality whereas the two on the "right" write about politics and current events. As a result, we provide neither counterbalance to the two on the right nor relevant articles for the day's political battles

It was one of the only emails to which I wrote a personal reply. This, in part, is what I said:

> On some topics, I imagine I am right of center; on others far to the left. I don't think that makes me a centrist. Indeed, I think that left vs. right is a race to the bottom that I want no part of. Far more important for our shared political future is our willingness to think independently . . . As others think for themselves, I like to imagine that they will end up rejecting the unimaginative, unthoughtful, and reactionary. If we prove ourselves unable or unwilling to think independently, then the larger social and political project of which the *Sunday Paper* is but a very small part is doomed anyway. And while we live in a time when rampant consumerism, ideological vanity, and media-fed intellectual shortcuts make independent thought ever more difficult (and even as education and spirituality—the historic centerpieces of those projects most able to resist such manipulation—grow frustratingly weaker), we are not yet doomed.

A year later, I find myself wrapping up a book that, though peppered with words like "politics" and "civic" is, primarily, a book written to educate readers about a particular way of being "spiritual." And as I read back through my editorials, I see that this is what I was doing most of the time, albeit in ways that I sometimes didn't see then and may disagree with now. In sharing the editorials, I hope I've modeled a practice of thinking and acting that is useful. I'm more confident than ever, however, that my editorials are not models to emulate. Some of them reveal the degree to which I failed to think for myself; others the degree to which thinking for myself wasn't an especially good idea. Some of them make points so specific to a particular set of events as to be of little use now; others make points so general as to be of little use when applied to any particular set of events. I can only imagine what I'll think of this book if I come back to it in ten years.

But isn't that part of the point of all these practices? That they're *practice*? That they're occasions in which we imperfectly repeat actions so as to get better at them without deluding ourselves into thinking that getting better at something means getting it perfectly?

Living publicly as if one's faith matters, letting hope shape one's worldview, loving God and neighbor: these, too, are practices. Even when trying (sometimes, it seems, especially when trying) we can be as faithless, hopeless, and bereft as the next person—though hopefully less often as we learn the lessons of regular practice.

While not dismissing the costs that come with inevitably doing things wrong, neither should we magnify those costs. There is, I think, a necessary playfulness that comes with practice—one that refuses to so dramatize our failures or trumpet our successes that we lose sight of the greater projects that constitute lives lived before and toward God. The coaches' old dictum, "You play like you practice" needs only minor modifications to fit such a life: You play because you practice. Or, said even more fiercely, you must play because you practice. The threat of risking failure and the burden of developing discipline otherwise feel too great. I tried to remind myself of the importance of play while writing editorials and at least once that reminder came out fairly literally: "Finding Sanity in March Madness."*

If nothing else, such playfulness reminds us that the world is far less under our control than we might wish and so whatever power or authority we inhabit we live in only loosely and temporarily. Not only do things change but our destinies are not ultimately captured (meaning both constrained and described) by the world. Indeed, the practices I've rehearsed in this book are a kind of training for a destiny which is richer and larger than our blinkered and partial visions now reveal. We make sense of a faith shaped by hope and driven by love as much by a tradition-informed imagination as by an independently-derived reason: imagining what will be, we treat our lives as rehearsal for it.

Because the world is so fluid and complex, our political engagements with it and those who journey on it will also be fluid and complex. This, I think, is part of what can make politics so frustrating: even our best solutions to the political problems we face are only temporary (because things change) and always imperfect (because we can't control so much complexity). No wonder politics leave so many so disillusioned. And no wonder it's so important to treat our political engagements as practice. In the face of the world's mutability and our finitude, there's nothing else we can allow it to be, lest we treat the defeats we so regularly suffer as final. Treating politics as practice is a kind of therapy against the psychic costs that come with either discovering that our hopes were unfounded or founding our hopes in the (eventually failing) promises of those who assure us that their vision can solve the world for us.

Yet if all we discover is that our political lives are simply too big for us to handle on our own, we have not yet discovered enough. Such a discovery projects us, ricochet-like, away from unfounded hope and into unjustified nihilism. The world becomes nothing but whirl, and practicing at politics becomes nothing but game-playing with no larger point to our actions. The danger in this is that when we tire of the game, we think we can quit without consequence. Treating politics as practice helps us resist such "it's just a game anyway" conclusions—which is good, since quitting as if politics doesn't matter can be as problematic as quitting because we can't win. When we surrender our political lives to those who promise to solve the world for us or we abdicate from the world of politics, we leave the world to those whose visions will collapse in on themselves or whose desires are for their own glory. While the world's complexity will eventually defeat both the promise-makers and the glory-seekers, their pretensions toward utopian fantasy or petty tyranny can cause enormous suffering in the meantime. Practicing at politics, therefore, isn't only therapeutically helpful; it's morally obligatory.

Part of the secret is, I think, to realize not only that our political lives are too big to manage on our own but that they are too small to contain our destinies. Christian vision begins with the wisdom that the world—including the political world—is good and that it matters: it is not only created by God but a place in which God continues to act. When Christians engage the surrounding political world, they ought to do so with the sense that they have been invited and commanded to participate in the world with God. We practice in political life because this world—including the political world—is a place of divine interest and action. The present world matters and politics are important.

Christian vision does not end with that understanding, though. It ends with a vision of the Kingdom of God that has been inaugurated in Jesus' incarnation and will come in all its fullness as the consummation of this present world—including this present political world—but has not yet fully come into view. God's actions in the world, therefore, are not simply for its governance but toward its transformation. When Christians engage the surrounding political world, they ought to do so with the sense that it cannot presently satisfy them. We practice in political life because we are still training ourselves to live in a world that is not yet as it will be. The present world matters but it is not our destiny and the political issues of the day are simply too small to allow ourselves to be engulfed by them. Christians passionately engage the world around them as we find it but do so with an eye to the horizon looking for the world that we pray is arriving each time we repeat the Lord's prayer: ". . . Thy kingdom come . . ."

As we engage the world, we discover that we, too, are not yet as we will be. Our beliefs, our thoughts, our visions, and our actions are not yet perfect and not yet of a piece (or, rather, because they are not yet of a piece, they cannot yet be seen as perfect).

It's a bit late in the game to offer an apology but I do so now, albeit in a tepid way. It may be that a reader has made it this far into the book continuing to labor under the conviction that the way we think and the way we act can be separated—that belief and worldview and practice, since I describe them in separate chapters, are divisible and, therefore, that faith and hope and love can be kept distinct as well. To such readers, I apologize: the heuristic convenience of my ordering the chapters by the virtues shouldn't be taken as a sign that the virtues can be separated from each other. Indeed, part of the power of treating faith, hope, and love as *virtues* in the classical sense of that word is that the language of virtues defies any neat breakdown between thinking, seeing, and acting. Our thoughts shape our visions shape our actions shape our thoughts shape our visions . . . And, as I hope readers have noted throughout the more reflective portions of this book, the ideas I advanced in writing my editorials not only had the effect of shaping me as a writer and thinker, but the act of writing those editorials re-shaped the ideas I carried into my work.

This shouldn't be surprising. We're always getting shaped by what we do. Sometimes, we do so consciously: bodybuilders lift weights to look a certain way; scholars read to think in new ways; people of faith pray not only to express belief but to believe. Whether we're conscious of it or not, though, our environments (or, more properly, the way we interact with our environments) shape us. Nothing makes us aware of this like practice. After all, when we practice at something, we concentrate on it now so as to develop the ability not to need to concentrate on it later: we develop muscle and mental memory. Done repeatedly, an action becomes ingrained. As I type, I don't think about where the letters are on the keyboard; I think about the ideas I want to convey and the words I want to use to convey them. After years of typing, my fingers almost move on their own. Or, rather, they did until I wrote that sentence. Now I'm thinking about where the letters are—and typing more slowly as a result.

One of the implications of the fact that we are always being shaped through our interactions with our environment is that people of faith are not in the process of shaping their beliefs so much as reshaping them. Aware of this as I wrote editorials, I wrote holding the position that my readers had various beliefs that were being shaped and that I was, therefore, in my own small way, contributing to that reshaping when they read my editorials. I wanted them, therefore, to read as practice—which is why I was not only glad to write weekly but more willing than most editorialists to run series of columns over the course of several weeks. Repetition in reading (or, rather, repetition in thinking about what we are reading) helps reshape beliefs. Talk radio hosts know this better than most and it's one of the reasons they return repeatedly to the same ideas and catchphrases again and again: they're using repetition as an aid to reshaping.

The question to ask, obviously—and especially in light of the talk radio reference above—is what motives are guiding this reshaping? Suspicion of outsiders? Distrust of other political parties? Evangelical fervor? Curiosity about the world around us? Compassion for the least well off? In a world in which no one's motives are perfect and many are horrid, even the best of motives can induce suffering, not only in the hearers/readers being reshaped but, by extension, in those around them as well. Those—like editorial writers—who wish to participate in reshaping the thought and actions of their audiences, do well to attend, as best they can, to their own motives.

Faith, hope, and love may have been the virtues I was most interested in promoting as I wrote but even those virtues can be (and undoubtedly were) misdirected when they are pursued for bad reasons. Recognizing that my motives were impure (driven by pride, vainglory, anger, curiosity, contempt, amusement, fear, panic . . .), I practiced—sometimes half-heartedly but nonetheless consistently—at being motivated by love towards those who would read my columns.

I was in good company in this. Christian theologians for centuries have bound the virtues of faith, hope, and charity together in a single larger motivating vision of Christian love: God's love shapes human faith, hope, and charity toward both understanding and activity. Likewise, treating faith, hope, and love as practices places them within a single vision large enough to encompass what we think, what we believe, and what we do. This vision is centered in God's love for the world and our worship of God as expression of and response to that love.

As a starting point, then, Christians might ask how participating in worship services shape them for engaging the rest of the world: what do they learn in those services, how do they act in those services, and how do the things they learn and do shape them to learn and act in the wider world? Beyond that, though, they might also ask how the fact that they are being shaped into certain kinds of thinkers and doers in worship services implies that—unless they wish to lead increasingly schizoid lives—their shaping in worship will have an impact on their thinking and acting outside of worship services.

Indeed, all this suggests a kind of grand test for the public practices that come with faith, hope, and love: can this action be understood as an expression of worship? Where the answer to that question is yes, our practices will increasingly reveal a faith worth having, a hope worth sharing, a love worth acting on. Where the answer is no, we return and practice again. What, after all, are all those people gathering in churches and synagogues and mosques and temples doing other than practicing? I'm merely pushing us to think about practicing at worship in places outside of worship spaces—about making sure that our worship faces outward.

When we face outward in worship—when we practice believing aloud—we will, I think, discover that faith, hope, and love are wrapped in gratitude—for all that we have been given, for all that we are, for all that we can do, for all that awaits us. The reader who emailed me with his frustrations about political balance singled out one of my editorials, in particular, as evidence that my editorials were insufficiently relevant. Named "Grateful for Thanksgiving,"* it came out—obviously enough—the Sunday before Thanksgiving. What I didn't say in my email back to him, I'll say now: perhaps it wasn't the most politically pointed article I wrote, but in a society tearing itself apart as it figures out how to live together, I think it was the single most relevant article I wrote.

Finding Sanity in March Madness

(Appeared April 1, 2007)

Among major spectator sports, the NCAA basketball playoffs are the most important events in America. I didn't say "favorite" or "most enjoyable." Those qualities are too subjective and, truth be told, I'm not even that big a fan of basketball. I've played many sports at various levels of competitiveness and I've never been part of a sport that turned grown men into crybabies faster than basketball. That soured me on the joys of hoops. I said "most important" because the NCAA basketball playoffs are about the only remaining widely popular sporting events that highlight those qualities of sport that not only can teach the virtues of citizenship but some of what it means to be human. That may sound like hyperbole, but consider:

- March Madness celebrates excellence without giving up a sense of egalitarianism. Small conferences get seeds, small schools make it to the show, and every year the slate gets wiped—well, if not *clean*, at

least cleaner. In the process, the playoffs celebrate success without so narrowing its definition that it can pertain to only one person or group. Bubble teams are celebrated for getting into the tournament. Cinderella teams are celebrated for upsets (Virginia Commonwealth over Duke, anyone?). Well played games are celebrated for their thrill regardless of who wins. As such, the tournaments affirm both stability and surprise, which are values constitutive of durable society.

- Although difficult matters of gender and race have never been absent from American culture and clearly aren't absent in the playoffs, during March Madness we can watch both men and women of many races compete without being overly drawn toward evaluating play based primarily on criteria that are properly foreign to competition. College basketball is one of the only sports going in which attention to both women's and men's brackets marks purists and genuine sports aficionados. And since college teams are more shaped by the philosophies of their coaches than the personalities of their players, the tendency to equate styles of play with race—which is just another subtle form of racism—is muted. In college basketball (as in American society) there are still enormous hurdles to overcome with regard to gender and race. But watching March Madness gives at least a hint that we may be moving in the right direction.

- In an era of professional excesses, college basketball values the amateurs. Indeed, the otherwise troublesome move of high school players straight to the NBA actually reaffirms this value. We rejoice in teams as much as players, determination as much as talent, and the thrill of the game more than the value of the paycheck. The Olympics are great but they only come along for only a few weeks every two years and increasingly attract professionals anyway. The discipline revealed by amateurs pursuing excellence reminds us that hard work is to be valued

for more than the money that it might bring.

- Among major spectator sports, basketball is the only one that can stimulate the spectator toward participation. Football may be more popular but pickup football is played by different rules than professional football. Hockey can't be played in very many places and requires more gear than football. Baseball requires a crowd. Soccer is still struggling to make it in the U.S. And while NASCAR may be the most popular sport in the United States, is this really the sport we want to celebrate? One made possible by internal combustion engines, thrilling by potential tragedies, and practicable only to those with enormous disposable incomes—and one in which athletes spend the entire event sitting? Basketball requires nothing more than a ball, an opponent, and a single, generally readily-available hoop. As national trends toward obesity continue, the very idea that we can get our butts up off the couch and go do what we're watching is wonderfully countercultural.

- The fascination with March Madness that stimulates office pool after office pool, when combined with its amateur and participatory nature, can remind us of the complex relationships between body, mind, and spirit that constitute human existence. In what other sporting event are so many people caught up in the pleasures and pains of historical analysis, future prognostication, and mathematical manipulation as this one? And apart from participation how else can we discover that some things can only be learned by doing and some kinds of knowing are only possible in embodied ways? We are becoming a culture driven simultaneously toward Manichean and Epicurean excesses: we confuse health with weight, refuse responsibility for our physical conditions, make fitness trendy, and have become more preoccupied with the effect of food on wellbeing and longevity than anyone since Adam and Eve. If you want further evidence of our Manichean and Epicurean sensibilities, consider: some of you reading this column think it's a fluff piece precisely because it's about sports. And others think it's the first thing I've written that is of any interest.

So enjoy tomorrow's game, but as you watch, remember: its lessons—and those of the last several weeks—extend far beyond such simple matters as competitiveness, team spirit, and sportsmanship.

Grateful for Thanksgiving

(Appeared November 18, 2007)

Thanksgiving is, seemingly, a pretty innocuous holiday. The Macy's Thanksgiving Day parade, turkey and fixings, football, and a food coma: not the kind of stuff to get worked up over. Nobody worries about gift-equivalency, provokes arguments about proper holiday greetings, or suddenly gets preoccupied with the status of their souls. Nobody has moral qualms about Thanksgiving decorations on public buildings or (thanks be to God) works themselves into a lather over a supposed "War on Thanksgiving." Aside from overcooking, overeating, and overexposure to relatives, there isn't much to freak out about—which, I suppose, is something to be grateful for in and of itself.

A bit of reflection on the whole project of giving thanks, though, suggests just how surprising it is that Thanksgiving is such a laid-back holiday. After all, the yearly reminder to be grateful challenges at least two popular contemporary American myths: safety and self-sufficiency. Why else would we mark the holiday watching sports (the penultimate venue for discovering the cruelties of contingency) and preparing to gift-shop? Being thankful means recognizing just how contingent—how unexpected and insecure—life is. Those who would make a life (or a world) free from the risks of unexpected harm would, one imagines, have trouble imagining how to think about the unexpected blessings that gratitude celebrates. Likewise, those who would see themselves as rising upward by the force of their pull on their own bootstraps would be more likely to see the benefits of their lives as deserved rather than gifts. Or to say all that differently, any holiday that celebrates a fortune both evitable and undeserved must confuse Dick Cheney and Ayn Rand.

Of course, one of the dangers of Thanksgiving is that allowing it to be a day set aside from others can tempt us to treat the virtue it celebrates as either unique to that day or best taken in small quantities. If, as essayist Danny Heitman observes, gratitude "challenges us to stretch our moral vision because, like all virtues, it's much harder than it looks," then creating a holiday for it becomes a convenient way of freeing ourselves from its demands for the rest of the year. Thanksgiving-as-holiday is the inoculation that keeps us from having to worry about becoming infected with the challenges of gratitude for the rest of the year. Or, to change the metaphor, Thanksgiving is like the birdhouse at the zoo: a nice place for a quick visit to see otherwise-harmless animals that, nevertheless, has double-secured doors to make sure the birds stay in once we leave.

Though that danger is real—as the yearly "we should celebrate Thanksgiving every day" editorials remind us—it may not be quite as tempting as those editorials suggest. Not only is it providentially situated between the holiday on which we teach children to live, like *A Streetcar Named Desire*'s Blanche DuBois, dependent on the kindness of strangers, and the day when we "officially" begin the complicated process of gift-giving and receiving, but its comparatively low-key nature makes extending it into the rest of the year less threatening. Having Christmas every day would quickly grow exhausting; repeated Thanksgivings we might be able to pull off.

Moreover, Thanksgiving is more than a chance to practice gratitude; it's an occasion for hope. It reminds us that the myths of safety and self-sufficiency aren't the only ones that underlie American culture, but are matched by myths about the importance of embracing—and being embraced by—a community that we didn't entirely choose; about how the abundance at our table ought to be matched by a generosity of spirit; and about how cooperation and mutual service, though tenuous and halting, are preconditions for our collective movement into the future. As long as those myths can continue to exert their pull on our gathered lives—which is to say, as long as Thanksgiving still feels like a holiday worth celebrating—the possibilities for a better tomorrow remain.

So Thanksgiving isn't only a day for giving thanks. It's a sign that the proselytizers of fear and self-interest haven't yet succeeded in their quest to disrupt the most worthwhile parts of the American dream or paper over the human psyche's recognition that we exist by grace. And that may be worth getting worked up over.

Happy Thanksgiving.

Index

vulnerability, 122–24
waiting. *See* patience
Whitman, Walt, 113
wisdom, 10, 37–39, 64, 95–96
worship, 173–74

Lightning Source UK Ltd.
Milton Keynes UK
UKHW01f1323100918
328641UK00002B/487/P